MANIFESTO

A radical strategy for Britain's future

Francis Cripps ● John Griffith ● Frances Morrell
Jimmy Reid ● Peter Townsend ● Stuart Weir

Pan Books
London and Sydney

First published 1981 by Pan Books Ltd,
Cavaye Place, London SW10 9PG
© Francis Cripps, John Griffith, Frances Morrell, Jimmy Reid,
Peter Townsend, Stuart Weir 1981
ISBN 0 330 26402 8

Printed and bound in Great Britain by
Richard Clay (The Chaucer Press) Ltd, Bungay, Suffolk

Contents

Preface 7

Introduction 9

1 Britain in the modern world 13

2 Global markets and Britain's decline 22

3 Power and wealth in Britain 31

4 The survival of class privilege 42

5 The law for the poor 59

6 The state and the people 77

7 Representative government in Britain 90

8 The cause of Labour 105

9 The way ahead 123

10 The immediate response to the crisis 133

11 A strong and open government 147

12 Common ownership and industrial democracy 166

13 From him that hath 182

14 Social services for all 198

Index 221

Preface

Manifesto has been a truly collective enterprise. All the authors have written at least one draft chapter. Every chapter has been extensively discussed among the authors and with friends in the labour movement. These friends have often provided drafts as well as advice and information. Every chapter has therefore been modified by being subjected to the collective process. The authors have, of course, had the final say. But that is not to say that they assent to every proposal contained in the book. There have inevitably been differences of emphasis and approach which have illuminated for us issues on which the movement must undertake further debate.

We owe special thanks to Robin Cook MP and Chris Pond. Robin Cook was originally one of the authors and made a major contribution to our early discussions. He wrote several drafts and commented extensively on other drafts. Unfortunately for us, Michael Foot appointed him front-bench spokesman on Treasury affairs at a time when our book was at its most demanding, and Robin had to leave us. Chris Pond, director of the Low Pay Unit, was asked to advise on our future tax and social policy proposals, and became fully involved in our discussions on the whole book.

The following friends and colleagues contributed drafts: James Curran, author of *Power without Responsibility*, on the media; Andrew Gamble, of Sheffield University, on postwar international politics; Christopher Hird, deputy editor of the *New Statesman*, on big business and the City; Chris Holmes, a housing and community activist, on housing; Martin Kettle, of *State Research* and *New Society*, on civil liberties; Jenny Levin, co-director of the Legal Action Group, on legal reforms; Henry Neuburger, of the Conference of Socialist Economists' London working group, on economic and industrial policy; Jennie Popay, of the Study Commission on the Family, on health; and Rick Rogers, education correspondent of the *New Statesman*, on education. All their contributions have been subjected to the collective process and they cannot be held responsible for the final outcome, but we owe them thanks for the analyses and ideas which they so freely gave us. Mike Cooley, of the Lucas Aerospace combine committee, Alan Evans, of the National Union of Teachers, and Martin Smith, of the National Consumer Council, have also given us useful advice and information.

We are also grateful for their advice, comments and information to Sally Baldwin, Fran Bennett, Geoffrey Bindman, Lesley Day, Vladimir Derer, David Griffiths, Mary Kaldor, Ruth Lister, Lewis Minkin, John Mitchell, Mike Reddin, Hilary Rose, Pat Seyd, Robin Simpson, David Stephen, Hilary Wainwright and Sue Ward. We have also depended heavily on the secretarial services of Rosa Baretto, who cheerfully took on much of the organizing work, and of Carole Allington, Janice Day, Catherine Fuller and Jill Sullivan. Francis Cripps and Stuart Weir have been largely responsible for editing the book, with timely assistance from Harold Frayman, of *Labour Weekly*, who took on extra research for us, and from Michael Williams, of *New Society*.

Introduction

In Britain we live in a democracy, and yet we do not govern ourselves. We watch sympathetically the struggles of peoples of the Third World to establish themselves as self-governing nations. We do not relate the struggles between these peoples and their undemocratic ruling élites, financed by external financial power, to our own circumstances. But the parallel is there: less open, less savage, but just as real. Britain is a member of a vast economic and political empire, known as the free world. Some of the member states elect their governments; others do not. It is free trade, not democracy, which unites this world. The postwar organization of international trade in the West, according to the vision of a frontier-free global market, has stimulated the development of huge multinational companies, run by self-appointed oligarchies. Their manufacturing, trading and banking activities range freely across national boundaries. Their policies are outside the control of national governments. A network of international institutions, like the European Economic Community and the International Monetary Fund, maintain and enforce the rules of this global market. In the free world, these institutions and the multinational enterprises they protect have the power to shape the domestic and foreign policies of countries with weak economies, irrespective of the wishes or interests of their citizens. In this sense, Britain has become a subject nation, unaware of its subjection.

In the first half of this book, we show how Britain's subjection has led to industrial collapse and mass unemployment, has reinforced the power of the ruling groups – and the state – in Britain, and has undermined postwar hopes for a classless, self-governing society.

Our aim is to see Britain become an independent self-governing country within the free world. Our argument is that Britain, by taking control of its own economy and trade, could secure full employment, bring about industrial recovery and restore the welfare state. Such a strategy represents a clear challenge to the postwar economic order of the West – and to our own ruling groups in the City of London and multinational companies, which identify their own interests with those of the global market. A Labour government which seeks to carry out these changes and to plan our future in the interests of the British people would need an unambiguous mandate from the electorate. We believe that such a mandate could be obtained. The Labour Party, in response to the movement of opinion among working people, is beginning to seek that mandate.

Three political parties in Britain today represent the existing international consensus. The Conservatives, Liberals and Social Democrats are united in seeking to keep Britain within this consensus, and in denying the right of an elected government to put the interests of its people first. Their position is often presented as internationalism versus a selfish nationalism. In fact, the citizens of many other countries are seeking to resist exploitation by precisely the same means that we advocate for Britain, and to establish an alternative international order within which self-governing countries can determine their own futures in agreement with others. The liberation of Britain by a Labour government would be a symbol of hope to these peoples. That hope would be much the greater if we were able to build upon the foundations of economic recovery a freer and more equal society with the ability to contribute towards the creation of a new international order.

We, the authors of this book, differ in many ways. Our common bond is a belief in the principles and practicalities of democratic socialism. We reject both the unrestrained individualism of western capitalism and the centralized communism of Eastern Europe. Democratic socialism seeks to build a society within which each individual is able to realize his or her talents and potential – not as in the rat-race of the private market, but so as to enrich the common good. Such a society would be cooperative and participatory, rather than competitive and authoritarian, with fellowship between equals as the principle of human relationships. In the second half of the book, we concentrate on exploring ways in which we might achieve a democratic socialist Britain. We identify traditions and values we can build on. But we recognize that the achievement of democratic socialism will not come easily or soon. It must come as the result of a mass movement from within society, not as a doctrine imposed on society. The Labour movement can give a lead. But a democratic socialist Britain can emerge only when the British people decide to change their own society.

By concentrating our attention on the future for democratic socialism in Britain we have inevitably had to neglect other important issues. We decided, in particular, that we should not set out an international perspective for the future – that can only properly be done through discussion with socialists in other countries. We hope that our book will be of interest and value to socialists abroad, and will contribute to discussion of how a new international order might emerge which could bring together socialist strategies in various countries in a common perspective to meet their differing needs.

Francis Cripps
John Griffith
Frances Morrell
Jimmy Reid
Peter Townsend
Stuart Weir

1 Britain in the modern world

No country's fall from international power has been more dramatic than that of Britain. Fifty years ago Britain controlled an empire containing one fifth of the world's population. Today it is a fairly unimportant member of the western alliance and the European Economic Community.

This change has profoundly affected Britain's development during the past thirty years and has altered the whole context of our society and politics. Traditionally Labour Party and trade union efforts to advance socialism in Britain have been conceived mainly in terms of our own class system and government. The challenge for socialists today is to evolve a political strategy which takes full account of the huge influence on our country of economic and political developments throughout the western world.

International and national inequality are inevitably linked. Colonial rule placed poor countries under western tutelage and prevented them from escaping poverty. The operation of multinational companies, in combination with western-dominated international, economic and political agencies and defence arrangements, is perpetuating that unequal world order. But the arrogant and grudging values of the rich are as powerfully applied to the working people and the poor at home as they have been to the Jamaicas and Turkeys of the less developed world. It is often forgotten that the institutions of inequality were bred simultaneously at home and abroad.

This chapter will show how Britain, and indeed the whole of Western Europe, has come under the sway of national and international agencies, companies and institutions. Much of the time we are scarcely aware of bodies like NATO, the western alliance, the World Bank and other international financial institutions, the international commercial banks, and multinational companies like ITT and Mitsubishi. Yet the civil servants, businessmen and financiers who run institutions like these, together with their counterparts in national governments and companies, form a large class of top managers whose beliefs and prejudices shape many of the crucial decisions of our time. More and more these institutions and their executives have come to form a linked network which moulds public opinion and constrains what governments can do.

The western world, of which Britain is one small part, is not effectively controlled by any one system of government. Strategic decisions are usually reached by a confusing process of international discussion and negotiation as politicians, civil servants, business executives and bankers travel from meeting to meeting in one country after another. Our Parliament plays only a very minor role in this process. Nor are British ministers or the Prime Minister particularly influential, and our national government rarely challenges the political, financial and business decisions which so much affect us.

The western alliance as a whole is no longer coping very effectively with the obvious political and economic problems of our times. Britain has already been suffering the consequences of this failure for well over a decade. As our industrial base has weakened, causing stagnation of the whole economy, our society has experienced inflation, a new growth of poverty and mass unemployment. In these conditions the very idea of social progress begins to seem utopian.

The response in the City, Whitehall and Westminster has been disastrous. Instead of trying to secure greater independence for Britain and tackling our industrial decline, the reaction of most government and business leaders has been to lock us more firmly into the international financial and trading system and to suppress, so far as possible, expressions of discontent at the consequences. We are endlessly told that the Common Market is essential, that free trade must be maintained, and that unprofitable industries must be closed down. We are urged to believe that unemployment and cuts in the welfare state are necessary because of past and present faults in our own society.

One of the most basic divisions in our politics today is between those who believe that Britain must adapt to the 'harsh realities' of the capitalist international system, and those who wish to challenge that system and secure national independence as the basis for rebuilding our economy and developing our society.

We are firmly on the side of a challenge to the international system and to managerial perspectives in Britain which uphold that system. How can such a challenge be made?

The main potential for securing national independence lies in our tradition of elected parliamentary government. This has a far greater legitimacy than any existing institution of international government like the EEC. Very few people would seriously doubt the right of our national government and Parliament, if elected and supported by a majority, to leave the EEC and negotiate a new pattern of international relationships for Britain. One issue with which much of this book will be concerned is therefore how we could turn the idea of national self-government into a reality. Only a truly self-governing Britain can make a positive contribution to a fairer and more ordered international trading system.

The postwar free world

Britain's central position in world trade and politics was steadily undermined in the second half of the nineteenth century and into the present century when other countries such as the United States, Germany, Japan and Russia built up their own industrial systems which overtook our Victorian industries in scale and technical modernization. The erosion of Britain's power was limited up to the Second World War by the continued existence of the empire. This helped to preserve markets for our industries and to make the City of London the most important financial centre of the world. But in fact Britain is only a medium-sized country in terms of population, it is relatively short of natural resources, and it long ago ceased to be the world's industrial leader. There was no reason why it should remain a particularly wealthy or powerful country in the long run.

By the end of the Second World War, Britain was in no sense, militarily or industrially, the equal of its allies – the United States and the Soviet Union. It was the two superpowers, not Britain, which largely determined the shape of the postwar world. The Cold War, arising from the conflict between the superpowers, divided the entire world into two separate spheres of influence, and the most crucial frontier of all was that in Europe. Thus Western Europe, including Britain, became closely integrated into an Atlantic alliance with the USA.

By the late 1940s the security and prosperity of Western Europe was a vital objective for the Americans. Their concern was to guarantee the unity of Western Europe and underpin their military strategy of containing the Soviet Union. To this end they established NATO and provided a huge flow of Marshall Aid.

At the same time American businesses and banks, greatly strengthened by the wartime boom, were determined to move into new markets around the world including those controlled by Britain. The American aim was a 'free' world with free markets. They instituted rules of liberalization through organizations like the General Agreement on Tariffs and Trade, the Organization for Economic Cooperation and Development and the International Monetary Fund to enforce a transition from pre-war and wartime economies, separately managed by national governments, to a new international economy in which American companies could freely compete for business and invest capital. This transition required that national governments should progressively give up their rights to regulate trade and control movements of funds in and out of their countries.

Britain's special relationship

For over a hundred years the British establishment, the group of the most powerful people in our society, has been composed mainly of financiers, top civil servants, industrialists and professionals including journalists, lawyers and accountants who worked for them. Modern bureaucracy has made the establishment less visible, more anonymous. But, as we show in Chapter 3, the class of 'top people' is still there, in the City and Whitehall, controlling large organizations and huge funds of money, influencing public opinion and negotiating with its counterparts around the world.

The British establishment, with roots in the empire, has for long been used to a world role. After the war, as the empire came to an end, this role had to be redefined. It was believed that Britain's worldwide financial and commercial interests required that a new, open international system should be established to replace prewar blocs and empires and that the United States alone had the power to ensure that this would be done. In the eyes of the British establishment it was time for the Americans to inherit the mantle of imperial responsibility and it was vital that British governments, from the 1945 Labour Government onwards, should be unflinchingly loyal to the United States. Thus Britain built up a 'special relationship' with the United States. Official foreign policy was not merely to accept the American view of the postwar world, but to support it with enthusiasm.

The price of this special relationship has been very high. It meant that Britain for a long time after the war kept up costly military commitments such as the British Army of the Rhine and a string of overseas bases in places like Singapore, Aden and Cyprus. It involved rearmament and sending troops to Korea and support for America's military intervention in Vietnam.

More widely, the special relationship meant that British governments put the alliance ahead of national interests.

The effect was to be seen from time to time in economic policy, for example with regard to sterling and, most recently, oil.

Most important of all, Britain's firm alliance with the United States shaped the whole course of Western Europe's and Britain's subsequent development. It gave rise to the new world of giant multinational companies, petrodollars, Eurocurrencies and the technology race, in which we now live.

Britain and Europe
During the 1960s Britain's loyalty to the United States made it suspect to those in Western Europe, particularly General de Gaulle, who wanted to develop the EEC as an independent force. But as West Germany and France built up a powerful position in international trade within the American-inspired system, the idea of Western Europe following an independent path of development faded. Britain was overtaken in terms of economic power by other European countries. The Anglo-American special relationship counted for less and American relationships with West Germany and France counted for more.

Britain's eventual membership of the Common Market in 1973 had meaning at several different levels. Perhaps the most important was symbolic. Inside the EEC, Britain no longer had the option of seeking a special position. The western alliance was consolidated; future bargaining within the alliance would essentially be between the USA and Western Europe as a whole. This is why the question of whether Britain should stay in the EEC is fundamental. Only if Britain left the EEC could it negotiate independently with the United States and with the rest of Western Europe.

Formally, Britain's membership of the EEC has meant giving up sovereignty on a range of issues, of which the most crucial are trade and industrial policy. The European community, not the British government, now lays down the terms on which imports come into Britain, including

18

the tariffs to be charged, and decides whether government aid to industry is legitimate. There are therefore also immediate and practical reasons why Britain would have to leave the EEC if our national government wanted to control imports and make a large contribution to the rebuilding of industry.

While the western alliance has been consolidated, it has paradoxically encountered increasing internal and external difficulties. One source of trouble, discussed in the next chapter, has been the mounting chaos of trade and currencies as money, goods, investment and technology are shifted ever more rapidly in a worldwide pursuit of profits. The other source of difficulty has been the gradual development of many parts of the Third World, reflected most acutely in control of oil by the OPEC oil-exporting cartel.

The rise of the Third World

The postwar world was largely divided between the western OECD/NATO countries (world one) and the communist bloc (world two). The former European colonies, which were gradually gaining political independence, and other countries, which were not industrialized, came to be known as the Third World. Nearly all Third World countries have become economically dependent on the West. The immediate attractions of this to their governments and emerging élites were western aid and access to western products and technology. But in most Third World countries, the benefits accrued very unevenly. All countries acquired at least the apparatus of modern government, with an international airline and airport, modern hotels and military hardware. But at the same time there has been spreading poverty, hunger, repression, violence and war.

Everything has now got more complicated. With the rise of OPEC and of newly industrialized countries, the Third World has begun to seem a less useful concept. The growth of dynamic industrial capitalism in many Third World countries like Brazil, Taiwan and South Korea receives less emphasis in our media than famine in Bangladesh. Their firms, often subsidiaries of western multinational companies, are beginning to develop new technology and to export machinery and capital goods as well as the textiles and toys we have come to expect.

All this is alarming to Western Europe, which has become particularly dependent on imports of oil and raw materials from many parts of the Third World. We cannot ignore Africa and the Middle East. We would like to give aid and export equipment for peaceful development. Instead we are alarmingly dependent on sales of armaments to pay for oil and raw materials, and huge numbers of people continue to live in poverty or even to starve in countries to which we sell arms. So long as Europe remains dependent on the Third World, it faces inescapable dilemmas. Thus if we continue to accept the system of global trade and exchange which was set up by the rich countries to protect their interests at the expense of poor countries we are bound to go on facing ugly choices about our relationships with the Third World.

This system of relationships, like Britain's relationships with Europe, is all part of the 'free' world concept supported by our own establishment as well as by the western alliance as a whole. The establishment is more divided on policies towards the Third World because the moral dilemmas are particularly obvious. But so far Britain has been one of those countries which has refused to accept the proposals of the Third World – or 'South' as these countries are often described – for reform of a system which no longer serves the interests of the West especially well, and certainly damages our own interests. Our companies, supported by government departments, continue with their drives to manufacture and sell arms, and to invest and earn profits, in countries where people are enslaved. They have no alternative strategy.

The case for national independence
The mechanisms of free trade and multinational business are destroying Britain's economy. Our present interna-

tional relationships lock us into destructive patterns of trade and investment in many other countries and commit us to supporting an anarchic 'free' world. The international system's prescriptions for our economy are deflation or devaluation. Our own ruling establishment is made increasingly repressive and hostile to social equality as it struggles to enforce acceptance of the unpleasant consequences within Britain. We cannot hope for major reforms from the official institutions of the EEC or the western alliance as a whole. So long as present relationships persist we are likely to see a continuous deterioration of our economy and society.

On the other hand, our Parliament and government, supported by a majority, clearly have the basic right to negotiate new external relationships which would give Britain more independence and self-government. We could leave the EEC. We could negotiate new trading arrangements with America and Europe. We could control movements of funds in and out of the country. We could express an independent view inside or outside NATO.

It is unlikely that the United States or Western Europe will be able to run the 'free' world effectively, even in their own interests, as power becomes more widely distributed around the world. All western countries have begun to suffer some of the difficult pressures with which other parts of the world have always had to contend. They will need systematic planning to stabilize their economies and they will eventually have to negotiate their plans with other countries and blocs.

Such needs are most acute in Britain. By embarking on independent policies, desperately needed to stem decline, Britain could help to show the way to a resolution of the appalling difficulties now facing the whole of the western alliance and the Third World. A strategy for independence must be the starting point for any hope of socialist advance in our lifetime.

2 Global markets and Britain's decline

The inflation, unemployment and industrial decline which have occurred in Britain are quite often discussed in purely domestic terms. They are blamed on faults of the government, managers, trade unions or even workers in general without any reference to events in the rest of the world and the pressures they have imposed on our industry and economy. In reality, Britain's worsening economic problems have been strongly conditioned by the economic system adopted by the western alliance as a whole. International technology, international markets, international rules and ideas are as much responsible for the good and the bad in Britain's postwar economic history as any particular merits or faults in our own institutions.

The economic system of the West is sometimes called 'advanced capitalism'. The term is not much help because it tells us little about the essential properties of the particular world we now live in. The international economy is in fact a complex system with vast networks of trade and finance and a plethora of institutions – companies, banks, governments and international organizations, like the EEC, OPEC, the OECD, the GATT, the IMF and the World Bank.

Free trade and free movement of capital

As stressed in the previous chapter, the present economic system has been the result of an extension of the American conception of mass markets and minimum government intervention from the continental USA to Western Europe and, ideally, to the rest of the world as well. The concept of a 'free' world founded on global markets has been the hallmark of the postwar period. The key principles have been those of free trade and free movement of capital.

From the start, American plans for the postwar world

envisaged that governments should progressively give up the right to control imports. This programme of trade liberalization was made a condition for Marshall Aid. By 1960 Britain and other West European countries had removed virtually all licensing of imports and by 1970 import duties and tariffs had been reduced in most cases to well under ten per cent. The whole of Western Europe is now a tariff-free zone for internal trade in manufactures; tariffs on industrial imports to Europe from the rest of the world are seven per cent or less. The result has been a huge expansion of the exchange of manufactured goods between all western countries. It is now commonplace in Britain that a large part of the machinery in our factories and the goods in our shops is made elsewhere. The same has happened, although to a lesser degree, in West Germany, France, Italy and the United States.

Following closely on free trade came free movement of capital. At first the main justification for this was the need to move funds to finance trade and to pay for investment which spread new technology. The freedom to move funds was accorded to 'non-residents' – foreign governments and companies which had brought money into the country – and to 'resident' companies pursuing overseas business opportunities. Eventually free movement of capital became a dogma. Now any individual or institution in Britain, as in many other western countries, is allowed to move funds abroad freely for any reason they like. Huge sums of money daily move from sterling to dollars, from German shares to British government securities, from bank accounts in London to real estate in California, in and out of gold, tin, copper or wheat at the discretion of company treasurers, millionaires, fund managers and central bankers all over the world.

The institutional consequences
The freedom of trade and capital movements has had extraordinary consequences. It has permitted the rise of multinational companies competing on a global scale and it has created an unregulated international banking system

borrowing and lending currencies all over the world. The new institutions have brought new, sometimes unstable, pressures to bear on workers, managers and investors. The power of governments to control their economies as a whole has been drastically reduced.

After the war western governments had reached a high point in their power to control the economic system. They were able to plan spending, investment and employment and to control trade, exchange rates and finance. Today almost the opposite is the case. Governments must have the 'confidence' of financial markets in order to carry out their expenditure plans. Trade, investment and employment are largely out of their hands. They dare not change the rules except when business and financial pressures demand change. Their main role is to explain to electorates why the logic of market forces must prevail.

The modern global economy is not run by international government institutions any more than by national governments. The IMF does not control international finance, nor does the GATT control international trade. The main function of such organizations is to police the system and enforce market rules, not to take responsibility for the outcome.

The technology race
Global competition has provoked a rapid development of technology. Any company which gets ahead with new products can cash in on vast, worldwide sales opportunities. Companies which fall behind find their existing products and factories becoming obsolete. Governments abet the technology race in the hope that their countries will derive some advantage if 'their' companies gain a lead. Governments have also fuelled the technology race by military contracts in pursuit of strategic power.

In this race the larger and more profitable companies often have a head start. They can afford heavy long-term expenditures on research and development; they can cash in quickly on successful development, using their widespread networks of factories and sales organizations. The well-paid bureaucracies of large companies are easily a match for those of governments. They often cope with the myriad of languages, national regulations and local cultural peculiarities with a fluency which the Foreign Office might envy.

The giant companies are bureaucratic machines dedicated to financial profit. This logic means that they must try to move production where labour is cheapest or most compliant. They must abandon old-fashioned plants where they have got into difficulty in favour of green pastures elsewhere where they can make a fresh start. They must not take account of social needs unless this augments their own income. Modern technology for social needs could be a liberating force to create abundance for all and to free men and women from arduous repetitive labour. But the technology race, run in the pursuit of profit, is in many respects destabilizing western society. Jobs are insecure. Even new investments become obsolete. Profits are unreliable. Governments compete for favour by offering grants or tax concessions and pick up the tab when unemployment rises and investments fail. The unstable, shifting flows of innovation and production leave a trail of dereliction, unemployment and government deficits in their wake.

The global financial market
Unstable technology and production, and the up-and-down fortunes of companies, governments and countries, combined with almost total freedom to move money from one investment to another, have produced a speculative global money market. Commercial banks provide the basic network for dealing in dollars, sterling, marks, yen, francs and other currencies from Wall Street, London, Frankfurt and Zurich to the West Indies, Hong Kong and Tokyo. The market takes in deposits from companies, governments, sheikhs, speculators, traders and gangsters alike; it lends to governments, companies, nationalized industries and local authorities all over the world. One country – Brazil – now owes something like $80 billion,

25

about 600 dollars per head of population, to the international institutions. The City of London is heavily engaged in this business. British banks have more deposits and loans in foreign currencies than they do in sterling.

The international financial system is not regulated by any government or central bank, nor even by the IMF. Probably the people who are nearest to controlling it now are OPEC investors who have hundreds of billions of dollars of securities to look after.

From the beginning of the 1970s western governments found themselves unable to dictate the values of their currencies and finally abandoned fixed exchange rates. Since then the value of currencies has depended on what is termed the 'confidence' of the market. Britain, in 1980, commanded confidence to such a degree that the pound became one of the strongest currencies in the world. Its high value made foreign goods so cheap and British exports so expensive that most UK factories had no chance of holding out against foreign competition. Nobody decided that this ought to happen. It was the consequence of an entirely unplanned system.

The end of government power over the economy

When early postwar governments still had powers to control trade and fix exchange rates, they were able to take a genuine responsibility for spending and employment. They could counter any tendency to recession by cutting taxes and boosting spending to keep up the general level of business activity. Or they could cut interest rates and make credit more easily available.

If high spending resulted in a trade deficit, early postwar governments could borrow money officially or use their exchange reserves to cover the deficit. If the trade deficit was chronic they could change the exchange rate to make exports more profitable, or even postpone liberalization of trade to slow down the growth of imports. Few people imagined that the general prosperity of an economy and the whole pattern of its development should be dictated, not by government policies and internal pressures, but by the requirements of international trade.

Yet the latter is what has happened. As international flows of money and trade increased, governments found the balance of payments almost impossible to control. Then they found that they could not boost internal spending without risking external deficits and loss of confidence. Finally they accepted the dominant role of the financial market and international trade. They abandoned commitments to full employment, cut their own budgets as and when necessary, and urged the need for 'restructuring' of economies to match the supposed dictates of the international system. The message to companies and trade unions alike became that they must do whatever the market system required.

The full extent of the shift of perspective has been concealed by a form of 'double-think' typical of our times. Governments have acquired a huge administrative role because of failures of the market system, not only providing basic services like health and education but also rescuing bankrupt companies and ailing industries. Then we have been told that the reason for failures of the market system was that government had too large a role. The fact that governments have given up crucial powers of intervention and have little control over the economy as a whole is ignored. Instead they have been blamed for trying to pick up the pieces.

World slump
Since the mid 1970s there has been a recession of spending with high unemployment in America and throughout Western Europe. The recession was provoked, specifically, by the 1974 oil crisis and, more generally, by lack of 'confidence' of financial markets in any institution, particularly governments, which wanted to borrow money to keep spending going.

The oil crisis happened because the West had become heavily dependent on the 'world market' to satisfy fast-growing energy demand. Instead of planning to meet the foreseeable problem of gradual exhaustion of oil reserves, western countries had taken cheap oil, used it wastefully and neglected alternatives such as coal. The seizure by the OPEC oil-exporting countries of control over their own oil fields from the multinational oil companies, and the subsequent price increases, helped to force the West to begin facing up to the huge readjustment of patterns of energy supply and use which must be made. It also brought some OPEC countries vast earnings of foreign currency which they cannot immediately spend. Their surplus funds, mostly invested in western banks and government securities, deepened the crisis caused by high oil prices. If these funds had belonged to western companies or governments, as they would have under the old imperial system, they would no doubt have been spent without much difficulty. The fact that the funds had to be borrowed if they were to be spent caused a major problem, since heavy indebtedness of companies or governments is not something that western financiers encourage. In the event, a large part of the OPEC surplus was borrowed, through international banks, by a number of Third World countries. Exports to these 'debtor' countries helped the West to pay for its purchases of oil from OPEC.

To get out of recession the West would have to spend and borrow more than it is now doing. Oil prices would rise even higher than they are now and OPEC's surplus funds would build up all the faster. Alternatively, the West would have to save energy and develop new sources of supply much more quickly than it has done so far.

But the West will not begin to recover from recession so long as its governments and companies are afraid to borrow. As it is, the bankers' preoccupation with 'sound' money has spread through the whole international managerial class. Instead of boosting spending they are engaged in a destructive process of cuts and closures, mistaking the symptom of dissatisfaction – inflation – for the underlying disease of stagnant production and income. It should be obvious that when production falls governments need to put up taxes, companies raise prices and trade unions seek wage increases, trying to protect incomes from the costs of recession. Western bankers, managers and governments think that cuts will bring about the collapse of defensive inflationary pressures. This punitive attitude has been the recipe for a general slump.

The crisis of the British economy
Long before the oil crisis, Britain was badly affected by the development of global markets because it lacked natural resources, its industries were old fashioned and its establishment was keener on playing a world role than on strengthening Britain's own industrial base.

The consequences of free trade have been the saga of our times. The control of most factories passed into the hands of huge companies, British or foreign, with worldwide operations. Imports surged in until a country which only twenty years ago was almost self-sufficient in manufactures, as well as supplying large export markets, has become the most import-dependent of all the larger industrial countries, seeing its own factories closed down and sectors of industry wiped out.

The deindustrialization of Britain has caused mass unemployment, held back living standards and started to bankrupt the welfare state. All parts of the economy have been affected, but the effects have not been uniform. The North has suffered more than the South. Industrial workers have suffered more than service workers, workers more than managers. At the top, most of the establishment has continued to enjoy its privileges, taking advantage of global markets to make money abroad and integrate into the new international management class.

Britain's industries failed in a strictly relative sense. Our factories became far more efficient than they had been before. Our technologists made a considerable contribution to worldwide innovation. Our companies operated quite successfully as multinationals, building up investments all over the world. But the standard set by international competition was a ruthless one and the problems caused by an initial failure to meet it compounded rapidly. Factories in Britain had a less dynamic home market, workers in Britain had a slower rise in living standards, the British government had less buoyant tax revenues than their counterparts in other countries. Business and investment tended to move out.

In the 1970s the general recession in the West made matters rapidly worse. International managers, lacking confidence in general, lacked confidence in Britain in particular. In 1976 bankers and financiers wanted huge cuts in public expenditure, and the pound started to collapse on the foreign exchange market. The IMF was brought in to negotiate with the Labour Government and impose the market's remedy. What Healey and Callaghan undertook with some reluctance, the Conservative government has made into a religion. Britain must be saved through the market mechanism, whatever the cost. There was no alternative.

During the 1970s as the extent of Britain's crisis became apparent, the labour movement realized that the establishment would not challenge the international system and was instead adopting the philosophy of cuts. Labour had to evolve its own alternative strategy, which will be discussed later on in Chapter 10. The political divide between Labour's thinking and mainstream policies has become more obvious. The battle over Britain's future has opened out.

3 Power and wealth in Britain

Who are the people who have brought about Britain's economic decline by locking us so firmly into the global markets of the western alliance? Why haven't Parliament or the government challenged this process and those responsible for it?

In this chapter we shall show that the key group of people who have ensured Britain's subordination to international markets has been the tiny group which controls most of our wealth. These people not only administer British industry and property but also have a powerful influence over our politics and government.

The heart of the concentration of economic power in Britain is in the City of London, in the hands of a small, closely knit class with public-school backgrounds and extensive international contacts. Beside this class, the trade unions are weak. Even the government runs risks if it tries to move against them. These, above all, are the people responsible for Britain's vicious circle of economic decline and its social consequences.

The City

The City of London is a collection of financial institutions and head offices of large multinational companies. The institutions deal in money and investment. It may be said straight away that most of them are successful in their own terms. The point we are concerned with is not the efficiency of the City in handling money but its role in the administration of British industry and its largely undiscussed political power.

The banks, pension funds and insurance companies in the City which manage most of Britain's money are effectively controlled by about one thousand people. Consider the example of pension funds, made up of contributions from millions of workers and their employers, now worth over £30,000 million and growing faster than any other branch of the financial system. About two thirds of the funds are managed by merchant banks or stockbrokers. A mere twenty City institutions manage forty per cent – about £13,000 million. A *New Statesman* survey found recently that around two hundred people had authority to decide the investment of two thirds of all pension funds. Some thirty insurance companies similarly control four fifths of Britain's £40,000 million insurance funds. The four big banks account for seventy per cent of Britain's bank deposits and loans (another £100,000 million or so of our money).

In industry, the last twenty-five years have seen the growth of giant corporations: it has been an era of mergers, takeovers and multinationals. Industrial power has been increasingly centralized and concentrated in fewer and fewer hands. In 1953, for example, the one hundred largest companies accounted for twenty-five per cent of total net output; in 1977, they accounted for forty per cent. These large companies are not all part of the City. Some are nationalized, some are foreign-owned and some are based elsewhere in Britain. Most are linked to the City in some degree. Their bankers, principal shareholders, advisers and analysts will be found there. As Sir Arthur Knight, former chairman of Courtaulds, pointed out:

It is too often forgotten that 80 per cent of our manufacturing industry is run by 400 firms in each of which three or four people are responsible for the key strategic decisions – say 1,500 at most. And in the investing industry (pension funds, insurance companies, etc.) I would guess that the number of key individuals is even smaller.

Some large companies are still dominated by single wealthy families or individuals, like Sir Arnold Weinstock, with enormous personal power. The individuals or oligarchies in charge leave detailed management to their subordinates. The men at the top are concerned with strategy-investment, mergers, alliances, public relations and politics. Some two thousand of them effectively dominate the whole British economy.

A ruling class?

The people who run City institutions and large companies come largely from the same, privileged social background. They are linked together both by family ties and by business connections. Studies by sociologists and organizations like Labour Research have shown not only that the majority of top people in the City and industry come from public schools, but that the proportion with such backgrounds has been increasing, and that it is more marked the higher one looks. An examination of the backgrounds of the 150 directors of the ten main insurance companies showed that one third had gone to one school – Eton – and more than half had been at Oxford or Cambridge.

Business connections show up, for example, in the practice of multiple directorships whereby each person sits on several boards. A study of eighty-five large corporations found seventy-three linked by shared directors. Companies as diverse as BP, Shell, GEC, ICI, BICC, Dunlop, Cadbury Schweppes and Hawker Siddeley are linked in this way. Or to consider one company at a time, eleven directors on the board of BP were found to hold thirty-nine other directorships between them in companies and institutions, including the Bank of England.

Business connections are particularly close in the financial world. Barclays Bank, Nat West, Commercial Union Assurance, Sun Alliance and the Prudential share directors, as do Lloyd's, Guardian Royal Exchange, Eagle Star, the Midland Bank, Hill Samuel and Hambros. The 150 directors of the ten main insurance companies mentioned earlier held no less than 1,543 other directorships, linking them to clearing banks, merchant banks and a wide range of other institutions.

Family connections through birth and intermarriage are pervasive. Many of the families involved have titles. A study of directors in twenty-seven financial institutions found that all directors bar one had aristocratic links.

Barings, the oldest merchant bank, had five peerages – Cromer, Northbrook, Revelstoke, Ashburton and Howick.

The personal and family connections of top people in the City extend into government. Some City directors are simultaneously MPs. Many have brothers, schoolfriends or cousins who are high up in the civil service. People from the City often move into government. For example, Barings have provided two Chancellors of the Exchequer and a Governor of the Bank of England as well as a Lord Chamberlain and Governors of India and Kenya.

The overseas connections of top people have been formed in a variety of ways. There are ties deriving from the imperial past, wartime associations, student friendships at Oxford or Cambridge, links formed by immigration from Europe and emigration to the United States and, above all, business relationships abroad which have grown enormously in the past thirty years.

Merchant banks and insurance companies in the City undertake worldwide business on behalf of British and overseas clients. Britain's large industrial and trading companies – her multinationals – produce all over the world. British American Tobacco, Britain's largest private industrial company, has eighty per cent of its production overseas: BOC, Reckitt and Coleman and the Wellcome Foundation produce over sixty per cent abroad. On average, the top fifty private British industrial companies produce more than a third of their output abroad. Their overseas production is three times as large as their exports from the UK.

Within Britain, the role of City directors extends to management of the media and the arts. They sit on the boards of television companies, newspapers, universities, the Royal Ballet, the National Theatre, the British Museum and the Royal Opera. Commercial television and newspapers are largely funded by advertising budgets under their control. The arts depend partly on their sponsorship. Such 'good works' renew the flow of knighthoods and peerages by which top people confirm top people's superior quality.

Top people's wealth

The personal wealth and income of top people is not easy to measure since it is tied up in complicated ways to avoid tax, and since in Britain individual tax returns are not open to public inspection even for research purposes. It has been estimated that the top one per cent of people in Britain own eighty per cent of privately held stocks and shares. In 1973, less than half of one per cent owned nearly sixty per cent of all the land in England and Wales.

Death duties have led to the break-up of some large estates. But the aristocracy is still thought to own eighteen million acres of land, and 200 titled families have retained estates of 5,000 acres or more – often much more. Where land is sold off by families, it is frequently acquired by City institutions.

The fees earned in the City would astound most people if they were widely known. In 1976–7 the top-bracket stockbrokers, jobbers and insurers earned an average of £65,000 a year each; the top solicitors earned £56,000 and accountants £52,000. Directors may receive hundreds of pounds for half a day's work. The best pay-off of all is the insight which those in the City gain about profits to be made buying an option, a piece of a forest, a share or any other of the paper investments in which they all have private dealings.

The studies of the Royal Commission on Income and Wealth show that the distribution of wealth in Britain has changed remarkably little in the past thirty years – or even since the First World War. In general there seems to have been some decline in the shares of the very rich (the top one per cent), to the benefit of the merely rich (the next five or ten per cent).

High rates of income tax and death duties have had little effect because loopholes have been kept open and vigorously exploited at the top. The City is expert both at making money and at avoiding taxes. Small wonder that it has used this expertise to help its own.

Financial decision-making

The small group of people at the top of institutions in the City and large multinational companies takes key decisions about the investment of Britain's financial savings drawn from millions of people's bank deposits, pension contributions and insurance premiums. The financial institutions own the vast majority of shareholdings in British industry and business – the most significant power of all in a private enterprise society. These top people arrange mergers and takeovers, injections of funds into business and property development; they often dictate factory closures and redundancies. The financial institutions now finance most major property transactions. These top people, then, wield enormous power over the everyday lives of people and communities – power that is the more effective for being remote and unseen. They are the creators both of national wealth and of jobs. On what principles do they make their decisions? Why have the effects of their decision-making proved so destructive?

The essential point to grasp is that decisions in the City and multinational companies are based on financial criteria and worldwide information on markets and technology, blended together with the instinctive social judgements and political biases of their class. They are not concerned with the welfare of particular communities in Britain, with the survival of particular factories or even with the general level of employment and income in Britain as a whole. When a particular investment or closure is contemplated, their job is to look at accounting figures, not social facts. Their judgements are not supposed to be influenced by whether the outcome will be beneficial or harmful in anything other than financial terms. In practice, accounting judgements are fraught with uncertainty and subjective opinions have to come in. The basis of the City's subjective hunches can readily be ascertained, since it is accurately reflected in the pages of the *Financial*

Times. Its obvious characteristics are deep suspicion of British workers, trade unions and the Labour Party, and unease about the uncertainties produced by elected governments.

The supposed objectivity of financial decision-making is the City's safeguard, enabling it to claim that it acts without political or social bias. The subjective element in financial estimates provides freedom of manoeuvre, making sure that decisions taken rarely conflict with the City's social prejudices. The fact that accountants' calculations can be used to dress up prejudices, and at the same time yield increasing wealth to the City itself, gives many top people the illusion that they really do know what is best, not only for themselves, but for the world at large.

The influence of the City on British industries in the last two or three decades has reflected both its financial criteria and its prejudices. The search for secure financial gain meant that the City would not underwrite longer-term industrial investment that companies could not finance out of their own current profits. This has been disastrous for companies and plants which got into difficulty. Precisely when they most needed funds to modernize and write off past losses, they were unable to obtain them. Instead, they had to cut back, hoping by closure to re-establish a 'viable' base. All too often even this harsh process failed. Closures cost money, destroyed morale and reduced the scope of companies' future operations.

Worse still, some City institutions followed their financial logic through to the point of actively intervening in industrial companies to force closures and get control of land and other assets which could be sold off. The most notorious example of such 'asset-stripping' was that by the firm of Slater Walker. Pension funds (such as those of Leyland workers) under Slater Walker control were used to take over companies in order to close them down. The pension funds often actually lost money as a result but Slater Walker's own executives and favoured clients gained. When part of Slater Walker went bust in 1974, the Bank of England stepped in. But the City is forgiving.

Slater, having been found guilty on fifteen counts of illegal dealings, has like many another before him now quietly returned to City life.

Given the way in which they dominate the British economy, the decisions by the British multinational companies about where they invest, site production and buy components, and whether they supply markets by producing in them or by trade, are obviously vital to Britain's future as a trading nation. The evidence is not reassuring. Overseas investment by British multinational companies has been increasing two and a half times faster than their investment in Britain. They tend to regard Britain as a valuable market rather than as a production base. A survey of the investment plans of British multinationals after Britain joined the EEC concluded:

UK companies are planning to service their new or expanded European markets mainly from continental bases. This, when coupled with the evidence that continental firms are servicing their UK markets more through exports than from production facilities in the UK, is somewhat discouraging for the future growth of the UK economy.

(*UK Industry Abroad*, T. Houston and J. N. Dunning, 1976.)

It is fair to say that Britain's compounding economic problems tend to make the chances of profit on industrial investment here less than in some countries abroad. Another study, recently published by the Bank of England, acknowledges that, as multinational firms operate internationally, they are more likely to be sensitive to 'relative changes' in the economic performance of the countries in which they operate, and to adjust both short-term and long-term investment decisions accordingly. Thus the logic of profit would tend to induce some shift of investment overseas. But the City's pessimism about British workers and fear of Labour governments have almost certainly made matters worse. Until recently, many foreign companies found that relatively low wages and generous government grants and tax advantages made Britain a good place in which to start new projects. The City rarely seems to have taken this view.

When it comes to Labour government the City seems to be seized by something approaching panic. In 1964 Labour's election victory prompted an instantaneous out-flow of funds. In 1974 it caused a collapse of the stock exchange. In 1976 the City lost confidence in the Labour Government and caused a collapse of sterling. While many foreigners admired Wilson's and Callaghan's skill in imposing wage controls, the City's very fear that Labour government might succeed led the institutions to refuse to invest in government securities except at sky-high interest rates.

The City's political role
Whether or not it is engaged in moving funds out of Britain in reaction to Labour, or moving them back when the Conservatives are in power, the City is permanently and deeply involved in British politics and government.

Its direct influence on government comes through ministers, MPs and top civil servants. In every government, even Labour ones, there have been ministers who were closely connected to the City and industry. Almost all the present members of the cabinet have been company directors. The Chancellor, Sir Geoffrey Howe, was in 1978 a director of Alliance Assurance, EMI, The London Assurance, Sun Alliance, Associated Business Programmes and Sun Insurance.

The City's links with civil servants are less prominent, although the new practice whereby very senior civil servants resign or retire into top jobs in the City and in industry has received some adverse publicity (for example, when Lord Armstrong, who masterminded the 'three-day week' confrontation with the miners, retired to become chairman of the Midland Bank). The truth is that top civil servants in the Treasury and departments of Industry, Trade, Energy and Defence are in constant contact with people in the City, working out the allocation of government subsidies and contracts to individual firms, coordinating the announcement of major new projects and closures, discussing the pros and cons of changes in

39

taxation and broader government policies. Formally and informally, they provide a network of information, opinions and pressures which links higher levels of the civil service with top management in the City. In the privacy of clubs and private dining rooms, who knows how many times a day the Official Secrets Act is broken? Who, indeed, does the pooled information and gossip belong to? Even a minister could often learn from a friend in the City some vital political intelligence that he or she had not picked up within government.

Quite apart from direct and continuous contact with MPs, ministers and civil servants, the City has a widespread influence on politics and government of a less direct kind. It feeds the media, journalists, commentators and television researchers with information. The research and publicity departments of banks and large companies present information at a time and in a form which backs up their chairman's 'line'. They write the chairman's speeches. The whole propaganda process is reinforced as top people listen to each other and read the columns of *The Times* and the *Financial Times*. The City is one of the most important influences on opinion formation in Britain. Most of us see only the spin-off, in carefully edited form, on television and in popular newspapers which top people hardly bother to read. Our opinions tend to be ruled by a beautifully orchestrated and highly distorted version of the truth.

Mass persuasion is reinforced by direct professional pressures on most of those who should, or do, know better. People working in public relations departments would lose their jobs if they habitually told the truth. Fortunately for them, it is obvious that their job is not to tell the truth, but rather to promote ideas and interests defined by their employers. Journalists who make a practice of telling uncomfortable truths run the risk of their editor's or proprietor's disapproval and of being cut off from their sources of information. Many journalists make their living from privileged briefings accorded to them personally by top people on a basis of trust. (This is ritualized in government through the 'lobby' system, by which the Prime Minister and ministers can brief journalists without the source of the information being acknowledged in the resultant media reports.)

Many thousands of highly educated professionals are employed to do research and to prepare 'news' and views in the City and Whitehall. Without this organized back-up most top people wouldn't know what to say in public. The political power of the City in the end derives from its ability to employ these people to persuade us all that we are living in the best of possible worlds and that, if things go wrong, it is mainly our own fault. This is why so many ordinary people accept and even favour the continuation of establishment policies and privileges. It is why, astoundingly, a democracy where all adults have the right to vote remains largely governed by a few thousand people at the top.

4 The survival of class privilege

In 1945, after sharing the hardships of war, the majority of British people voted for a Labour Government to carry through fundamental reforms which would lay the foundations for a just society in which class privilege and inequality would fade away. The welfare state was the result of that election.

The wartime coalition government had already accepted commitments to a 'high and stable level of employment', introduced family allowances, and passed an Education Act making secondary schools available free to all children. And after Labour lost power in 1951 the Conservatives broadly accepted the welfare state which Labour had set up. A new consensus was established, which came to be known as 'Butskellism' – a term amalgamating the names of Rab Butler, the liberal Tory Chancellor of the Exchequer, and Hugh Gaitskell, Labour's social democratic leader from 1955 onwards.

From the viewpoint of top people, the consensus was a formula for social and political stability. It committed the leaders of the Labour Party and trade unions to accept a strategy of piecemeal reform. It provided an agent of social control – for example, through social security rules which reinforce the work ethic and women's dependent role in the family. It enabled the more wealthy and powerful members of our society to claim that they contributed most through taxation and to claim that, as managers, they were administering for a common good.

The claims for the consensus were not entirely hollow. The postwar Labour Government had established the national health service on the principle of free and equal treatment for all. It had set up a comprehensive national insurance scheme with flat-rate benefits which gave people a minimum level of income to help with most of the foreseeable crises of life. During the 1950s and 1960s

Britain largely shared in the prosperity of the West. Living standards doubled. Almost everyone became better fed, better housed and better educated.

But the consensus did not end the dynamic of social inequality. Progressive taxation was not fully enforced. Loopholes and avoidance practices spread, enabling the managerial and professional class to retain major privileges. Private and company welfare schemes benefiting the better-off were assisted and encouraged by legislation. The commitment to redistribution subtly changed. It was argued that public spending and benefits for the poor could only be financed out of economic growth. When, in the 1970s, economic growth faltered and eventually came to a halt, the welfare state was branded as an unproductive burden on productive industry. Finally, it was said by the Conservatives to be the *cause* of Britain's economic crisis. Too much taxation and public spending were alleged to have destroyed incentives and put mechanisms of wealth-creation out of action.

Briefly, in 1974, it seemed that the newly elected Labour Government might withstand these trends. The government maintained high public spending, introduced food subsidies and improved social security benefits. But in 1975 and 1976 cuts began to be made, under intense pressure from the City, culminating in an agreement with the International Monetary Fund which envisaged, for the first time since the war, absolute reductions in social programmes. Many members of the cabinet subscribed only reluctantly to the cuts. But most had come to believe that unemployment was inevitable and that electoral advantage lay in reducing taxes rather than in sustaining the 'social wage'. Roy Jenkins, who had been Home Secretary in the Labour Government – and is now a leading Social Democrat – actually argued that high public spending was itself a danger to freedom.

The postwar consensus, having been undermined by the confidence of the managerial and professional class in claiming its privileges, was ultimately destroyed by worsening inflation, rising unemployment and failures of economic policy. The Labour cabinet was not prepared to undertake radical measures to deal with the underlying deterioration of the economy. This is the reason why they were unable to resist City pressures and were forced to start cutting the welfare state. The consensus had served its turn. As it was undermined, so the hold of the establishment on Britain's managerial institutions had been reinforced. The proliferation of perks, private pensions and legalized tax avoidance extended the patronage which those at the top of public and private bureaucracies could offer. The managerial and professional class, benefiting from this patronage, remained loyal to their superiors and lost faith in the earlier postwar vision of an end to class.

Inequality in Britain today

The pattern of inequality is partially obscured by myths bequeathed to us from the days of Butskellism. Surely our tax system is progressive. The top personal tax rate, after all, is still penal. Capital transfer taxes and capital gains taxes continue to harass the wealthy. Only a few years ago, a Labour Chancellor, Denis Healey, promised 'to squeeze the rich till the pips squeaked'. And we are endlessly told that differentials have been eroded and that high incomes have suffered most from inflation.

The true position cannot be established with complete accuracy. Official statistics are nowadays badly distorted by tax avoidance at the top end. Much executive income takes the form of perks and benefits which do not have to be declared for tax. Money is paid into trusts. Homes become 'expenses'. Nevertheless efforts have been made to tabulate the distribution of reported income, before and after taxes and social security benefits. These figures show inequalities which have changed little in the past twenty years.

Typically, the reported earnings of the top twenty per cent are two to three times as high as those of the great majority, and this discrepancy is only slightly narrowed by the tax system and social security benefits. The differential extends into retirement. The top twenty per cent of retired people have about as much private income of their own as normal families of working age and on top of this they have very considerable wealth to run down.

On the other side of the scale, the bottom twenty per cent of families of working age have half, or less than half, the earnings of the majority. And all retired people, bar the privileged twenty per cent, have virtually no income of their own at all. These are the families and pensioners who have to live off social security – at an income level about half that of 'ordinary' people of working age. For the poor, subsidized housing, free education and, even more, the national health service are crucial. Such benefits add about forty per cent to their effective income. Apart from the very rich, Britain might be described roughly as a 'one/two/four' society. Taking the basic income level provided to the poor as one unit, 'ordinary' families are *twice* as well off. The five million or so middle-class families who constitute the top twenty per cent are *four times* as well off (more, if wealth and fringe benefits could be adequately taken into account). Right at the top, of course, is a stratosphere of people who are many times richer again. Class divisions are founded on this inequality of income and they reinforce it. Conservatism finds its hold on people through the anxieties which major inequality perpetuates. People all too easily hope to join the ranks of the privileged and fear the depression of poverty. The moral challenge to our society ought to be to overcome division. But in practice our institutions of government and business are continually reinforcing it.

Private welfare

The privileges of the managerial and professional class are buttressed in three ways. They receive high salaries or fees, pensions and fringe benefits from the organizations for which they work. They benefit from owning their own houses and having a certain amount of financial wealth. And they can take advantage of tax concessions on mortgages, life assurance, private health schemes and other pillars of middle-class status encouraged by the tax laws.

Home ownership is a good example of the way inequality is reinforced. Since 1963 owner occupiers have paid no tax at all on the rental value of their property. On top of this, if they finance their home with a mortgage they get tax relief on interest (which, being generally less than the rate of inflation, is effectively a capital repayment). People who can once get started with an expensive house find in effect that it costs them nothing at all. The catch is that you have to be quite well off to get started. You need a deposit of several thousand pounds and enough income or wealth to meet heavy initial interest charges in the first few years before inflation catches up. Many companies and institutions help their executives with such initial problems by lending them money on ludicrously favourable terms. From then on, the tax system picks up the tab on their behalf. After ten years or so, they have acquired a valuable property and paid off most of the debt at very little cost to themselves.

Virtually all professional and managerial families are home owners. Less than one quarter of working-class families are in this position. The value of the tax exemption on the rental value of owner-occupied properties is not even officially estimated (though independent sources put it at £2,000 to £3,000 million). The cost of the tax relief on mortgages is huge, again about £2,000 million, and in 1979 over one third of this relief was taken by fewer than one tenth of taxpayers, all earning over £10,000.

Occupational pension and sick-pay schemes are the two most significant of the expanding range of benefits which companies provide for their employees. Pension schemes come in a wide variety of forms and scales. Apart from those in the public sector, they are predominantly the prerogative of men in non-manual occupations. Private pensions carry inequalities of income during people's working lives into their old age. The better paid the job, the more likely it is to carry a pension. The better paid the worker, the higher the pension becomes. While ninety per cent of non-manual members of private pension schemes have their pensions based on final salaries, only two thirds of manual workers enjoy the same privilege. The tax advantages which attach to private pensions encourage companies to give very high benefits to top employees – for pension schemes defer earnings to future years of retirement when these employees will probably be paying less tax. The pay-off is further enhanced by payment of tax-free lump sums on retirement. It was officially calculated recently that an executive paying the highest rate of tax (then 83p in the pound) could reduce the rate to 62p in the pound by taking advantage of these reliefs. Like private pensions, sick-pay schemes also favour highly paid non-manual workers and discriminate against manual workers (especially women). At the latest count, eight in ten employees were covered by company sick-pay schemes. But while nine out of every ten non-manual male and female staff were protected, only three quarters of male manual workers and little over one half of female manual workers were covered. Additionally, while benefit is paid from the first day of sickness for nearly all non-manual staff, a considerable proportion of manual men and women workers are not entitled to receive sick pay immediately. There is a similar bias in the amount of sickness benefits, and manual workers are far more likely to have to serve a qualifying period in employment to be eligible at all.

It is 'perks' which demonstrate class advantage most openly. The Royal Commission on the Distribution of Income and Wealth described two main groups of such benefits. The first group were provisions – like free or subsidized meals, rent-free housing, sports facilities, and goods at discount prices – in principle available to most or all employees of the firm. These have increasingly been negotiated with trade unions as a way round wage restraint. But even these benefits still reflect class differences. Take subsidized meals as an example. Directors and managers are far more likely than manual and clerical workers to receive a free meal or a large subsidy and the quality of the food provided to them is much higher. Meals in company canteens and dining rooms are tax free. On this count alone they are worth more to executives on high rates of tax than to workers on the standard rate of tax.

The second group of perks are those reserved to managers only. They include full use of a company car, assistance with house purchase, free medical insurance, free or cheap loans, profit sharing and share option schemes. There has been a significant growth in these fringe benefits, especially under the last Labour Government. They have two ostensible justifications. First, they are supposed to make up for a narrowing of differentials between executive salaries at the top end of the income scale and wages at the bottom end. This 'justification' hasn't even the merit of accuracy. There has not been a significant narrowing of the income scale in the recent past. Secondly, fringe benefits were said to be a compensation for income policies. The latest survey by Inbucon, the management consultants, of managers' pay and benefits shows that executives achieved a gain of eleven per cent in real terms (on top of rises swallowed up by inflation) during the last years of the Labour Government. And yet more and more people in managerial positions improved their fringe benefits. Take the rise in use of a company car. By July 1980 nearly three quarters had a car, the biggest jump having occurred in the second year of Labour's incomes policy. The likelihood of having a company car increases with salary (eighty-six per cent of managers earning over £10,000 a year receive the use of one). The type of car varies with status too. A company director would typically be given a Rover while a salesman drove a Ford Escort. The use of a company car is normally worth several thousands of pounds to a well-paid executive. It is now taxed, but only on the most notional scale. Free private medical insurance through BUPA and other schemes has also grown fast and now covers a majority of high-paid executives. Private companies have been the main force behind the large jump in private medical insurance. Although much publicity has been given to group schemes for skilled manual workers like the electricians, access to private health care is still largely confined to professional and managerial employees and their families. Life assurance – usually used to fund superannuation and medical insurance – peaked in 1979 when two thirds of high salary earners had premiums paid through the company. Overall, the value of fringe benefits and superannuation to the average managing director is believed to have increased from about twelve per cent of salary (£2,500 a year) in 1974 to thirty-six per cent of salary (almost £11,000) in 1980.

We have shown in the previous chapter how public schools dominate access to the very top positions of power and wealth in British society. This gateway is overwhelmingly monopolized by the privileged class for its children. Analysis done for the Oxford social mobility study shows that two thirds of children at élite public schools (Headmasters Conference schools, which include Eton, Harrow, Winchester and Charterhouse) come from middle- and upper-middle-class homes (one seventh of the population). Only a minute fraction have manual workers for fathers. Similarly, the children of professional and managerial parents have taken up half the places in direct-grant schools and nearly half those in other private schools. The parents of these children buy educational as well as social and occupational privilege. Public schools have lower teacher-pupil ratios, well-stocked libraries, modern laboratories and ample playing fields. By contrast, the government's secondary school survey in 1980 showed that two out of five state secondary schools had deficient laboratories and that cutbacks in public spending had resulted in grave and widespread deficiencies in books and teaching materials. Children from private schools are six times more likely than ordinary secondary school children to go on to university. Half the undergraduates at Oxford and Cambridge come from private and direct grant schools. (There is evidence that they gain entrance on A-level examination scores which are, on average, lower than those of entrants from state schools.)

The cost of private welfare

Owner-occupied housing, company pensions and perks, life assurance, private medical care, and public schools all receive, in diverse ways, subsidies from the state. We have already described how tax allowances and reliefs underpin home ownership, occupational pensions and other benefits which primarily advance the well-being of the middle and upper middle classes. The last Labour Government acknowledged that these allowances and reliefs should be regarded as 'tax expenditures' akin to public expenditure, since they represented lost tax revenue. But while the Treasury has imposed strict control on public expenditure on housing, education and other social services through budgetary planning and 'cash limits', it was obliged to acknowledge that it could only estimate the growing cost to the Exchequer of tax allowances and exemptions. Tax reliefs are an open-ended commitment over which government has no ongoing control. The government has published estimates of the cost of some 'tax expenditures' in recent white papers on public spending. In 1979, for example, owner occupiers received an estimated £1,450 million in mortgage tax relief and a further £2,000 million in exemptions from capital gains tax. In the same year, general subsidies for council housing amounted only to £1,990 million. Reliefs on life assurance premiums cost £430 million. Pension schemes took an estimated £500 million, but the 1979 white paper acknowledged that this does not represent the full cost.

The very purpose of the recent growth in company benefits has been to substitute income in kind for taxable income, so reducing the tax liability of the highest-paid executives. Many company benefits, like 'bridging loans' and free meals, are entirely free of tax. The use of a company car is only notionally taxed. The cost to the company is counted of course as a business expense.

Firms which pay private medical insurance for their

employees can count the cost of those subscriptions as business expenses, but the subscriptions are counted as part of the employee's taxable income. However, private medical insurance and care receives substantial public subsidies in other ways. BUPA and the other provident associations escape taxation. They are registered as non-profit-making insurance companies and they put their 'excess of income over expenditure' into a general reserve, or invest in charitable trusts which own and are expanding private hospitals and nursing homes. Private health lives like a parasite off the national health service. It relies almost entirely on doctors, nurses and other staff trained in the NHS, and it has access to costly, publicly provided facilities.

The public schools are also heavily subsidized by the state. Annuity trusts, life assurance and other tax avoidance schemes reduce the cost of fees for families who send their children to independent schools. The schools themselves possess charitable status which carries tax exemptions and rate reliefs. The largest state subsidies to private education are in the public provision of free or subsidized places in independent schools and the training in the public sector of the majority of their teachers. Overall, it has been estimated that in 1979 these subsidies amounted to at least £350 million and probably cost over £500 million.

The myth of progressive taxation

The last Labour Government raised the highest rate of income tax to 98p in the pound. The Conservatives have since reduced it to 75p in the pound. The existence of these apparently penal rates of tax has created the illusion that Britain has retained a severely progressive tax system which has soaked the rich to meet the growing demands of government expenditure. In reality, both Labour and Conservative governments have allowed wealthy individuals and private business steadily to reduce their contribution to tax revenue and have increased the tax liability of ordinary workers at lower and lower levels of income to make up for the loss. In 1949, for example, taxpayers with the highest incomes (the top ten per cent) contributed nearly three quarters of all income tax collected. Thirty years later they paid only one third of the proceeds of income tax. It is true that the top ten per cent's share of total income fell over the period (from thirty-three to twenty-six per cent of all pre-tax income), but only a minor part of their diminished tax contribution can be attributed to their smaller share of income. Their share of income is now scarcely diminished by direct taxation: in 1977, it was twenty-six per cent of all pre-tax income and twenty-three per cent of all post-tax income. In the same year – when tax was apparently being levied at a fearsome 98-per-cent rate at the upper reaches of the income scale – the very richest one per cent contributed less than half their reported incomes in income tax, and the top ten per cent under a third.

How has this come about? The answer lies in an unequal erosion of the part of income on which tax is actually levied. In the late 1970s, almost sixty per cent of all 'taxable' income escaped tax through allowances and avoidance. The British tax system is riddled with allowances and exemptions. Taxpayers are allowed to deduct two main types of allowance from their taxable incomes, paying tax only on what is left over. One is allowances on various kinds of expenditure. Most working-class taxpayers have been unable to make use of these as they reflect a way of life and opportunities which are predominantly the preserve of the middle class. Thus, expenditure on mortgage interest qualifies for tax relief but rent does not. Life assurance and superannuation contributions can be offset against tax but national insurance contributions cannot. Fees to professional bodies are exempt but trade union subscriptions are not. The other type of deduction from taxable income is personal allowances, the most familiar of which are the single person's allowance, the married man's allowance, and the wife's earned income allowance. These are supposed to allow for personal circumstances which might reduce a taxpayer's ability to pay tax. In 1979 they were worth twice as much to the highest income taxpayers as they were to a standard-rate taxpayer and they cost the Exchequer over £12,700 million.

Tax avoidance has been of great significance in protecting the extreme concentration of wealth in Britain. Prewar gift and inheritance taxes contributed fifteen per cent of taxes collected, but in the subsequent forty years their share has run down to a mere 1½ per cent. In 1975, the government introduced a capital transfer tax to replace the old estate duty which had become so riddled with loopholes that the Inland Revenue described it as 'voluntary'. But the new tax was gravely weakened by a series of concessions and at the end of Labour's term of office it was actually raising less cash than the defective estate duty had in 1974. Labour was pledged to introduce an annual wealth tax in 1976. This was not especially radical – a dozen OECD countries already have a wealth tax. But the parliamentary committee set up to work out the details of such a tax produced five contradictory reports, and the government took the opportunity to neglect the commitment, in spite of efforts by the TUC and Labour Party to revive it. Paradoxically, inequalities of wealth increased under Labour (largely because of a rise in asset prices) while the revenue from taxation of wealth fell by half.

The tax base has been further eroded by the decline in the share of tax paid by private companies since the war. In 1946, companies contributed nearly a fifth of total government revenue. But while other types of taxation were increasing in real terms, the effective tax rate on companies fell by more than half between 1953 and 1973. By the mid 1970s the corporate sector in Britain contributed far less than in most other advanced industrial nations. In 1974, the Labour Government introduced 'temporary' stock relief to bail out ailing companies. This proved to be permanent and has now nearly eliminated corporation tax for most companies. In 1979, it was estimated that eleven of the twenty largest companies (among them Allied Breweries, Courtaulds, GKN and Rio-Tinto-Zinc) paid no mainstream corporation tax at all. This was not because they made no profits. Between them, the eleven companies made an estimated £1,275 million. The top twenty companies paid only £388 million between them in 'mainstream' corporation tax that year – just 7½ per cent of their total estimated profit of £5,000 million. These industrial giants, therefore, paid tax at little more than a third of the rate paid by the average manual worker.

The shift in the tax burden

The falling contribution of companies and rich individuals to the government's budget has inevitably meant a huge increase in the tax liability of working people. Since 1945, the taxpaying population has increased from 13½ million to over 21 million people – much more than the growth of the workforce. Ordinary working people have had to bear a heavier share of tax at lower and lower levels of income. Take, for example, the position of workers on average earnings. In 1949, a single person on average earnings would have been allowed forty per cent of income tax-free; in 1979, the same worker would have begun paying tax at one quarter of average earnings. In 1949 a married couple with two children only began paying income tax at around average earnings and with four children did not pay tax until they earned much more. In 1979 such families started paying tax at less than half average earnings. There has in fact been a shift in the burden of income tax from single people and couples without children to taxpayers with children. The share of income paid in tax has increased more for families with children than for other taxpayers and, remarkably, the larger the family, the larger has been the increase.

Even the poorest workers now pay income tax. The tax threshold has fallen below the supplementary benefit poverty line – which represents a bare subsistence level of income. In 1979, four out of five families who were officially deemed poor enough to qualify for family income supplement found themselves obliged to pay all or part of the supplement back to the government in income tax.

54

The position of the poorest taxpayers was additionally prejudiced by the fact that the rate at which they begin to pay tax was increased to 35p in the pound under the Labour Government. Even now, at 30p in the pound, it remains the highest starting rate for low-income taxpayers in the world with the exception only of Australia. This high rate of tax has sharpened the bite of a phenomenon known as the 'poverty trap'. The overlap of tax and national insurance deductions with eligibility levels for means-tested benefits like rent rebates has created an absurd and unfair position in which low-paid workers can actually lose from wage increases (higher tax and national insurance deductions and reduced benefits outweigh higher pay). Over a wide range of earnings – from £40 to £100 – workers with families end up with roughly the same net income in take-home pay and benefits, whatever they earn. Wage increases for them vanish into thin air.

Labour's crisis of commitment

Labour was elected to government in 1974, committed by the party's manifesto to bring about a 'fundamental and irreversible shift in the balance of wealth and power towards working people and their families'. There were signs of radical resolve and egalitarian commitment among ministers. In March, three weeks after gaining office, Denis Healey, the Chancellor, reasserted Labour's election pledge in the House of Commons and announced tax changes designed, he said, to 'ensure that the rich bear a higher share of the tax burden than they have under the last government'. In the election campaign in October 1974, Tony Crosland stated that 'we are determined to stop this situation where the richest men in our society get their houses cheap'. The opposition of unions in the health service towards private pay-beds strengthened Barbara Castle's resolve to carry through Labour's policy of clearing them out of NHS hospitals.

We have already seen how the City and the international financial community forced the Labour Government to abandon its public spending plans and the fundamental commitment to full employment. The abandonment of Labour's interventionist industrial strategy similarly left the government with no alternative but to seek to revive the confidence of the top management in private industry. The price was high. The government accepted management's case for 'restored' differentials while at the same time imposing wage restraint on the majority of workers. In March 1977, Healey introduced a budget which gave away to a family on £25,000 a year nearly *ten times* more than to an average wage-earning family. In his budget statement, Healey apologized as follows: 'I should have liked to do more for those at the bottom of the earnings scale. But I have felt it necessary to concentrate relief where it is most needed.' In other words, Healey had put the government's election policy into reverse. The very managers Healey was seeking to propitiate were already displaying remarkable ingenuity, through company perks and tax avoidance, to avoid even relative hardship. Far from cracking down on tax avoidance, the government issued gilt-edged stock on terms designed to help people seeking to avoid higher-rate income tax. The government was, of course, sensitive to the growing unpopularity of income tax among working people. But given its strategy of appeasement, the government was unable to relieve their growing tax burden by shifting it on to the broader shoulders of the rich. Cuts in public spending were therefore continued in order to make room for cuts in income tax. And there began a retreat from direct taxation to indirect taxes (like VAT) which by 1979 raised over a third of all government revenue. Indirect taxation is regressive: that is, it takes proportionately more from ordinary workers than it does from the rich. But it also takes its share of people's incomes less obviously. It is for these two reasons that the Conservative Government continued the shift away from income tax.

We have explained that neither Labour nor Conservative governments acted to mitigate or remove the 'poverty trap' despite its blatant injustice over a wide range of below-average earnings. But this is not to say that the last Labour Government was not sympathetic to incentive arguments. Take the case of mortgage tax relief. During the 1960s, the Labour Party – Left as well as Right – allowed the government to woo electorally powerful owner occupiers and relegate council housing to second-class status. Private housebuilding even overtook public housebuilding, and many ordinary families have been forced into an owner occupation they have not readily been able to afford. But by 1974 the party had reasserted the importance of public housing and wanted to put renting and owner occupation into some kind of financial balance. Labour was committed at least to abolish mortgage relief at the higher rates of tax. But after an agonizing long-drawn-out housing finance review, the government came down even against this modest measure of equity. The £95 million which in 1977 went in relief to the richest house-owners was spared in the cause of incentives to management. Needless to say, there was no thought of limiting mortgage tax relief in general, let alone any of the other tax allowances which underwrite the private welfare of the middle class. The housing finance review showed that the huge bounty of mortgage tax relief would swell by two thirds over the next ten years. But the government justified its retention in this classic statement of conservative doctrine:

We certainly do not believe that the household budgets of millions of families – which have been planned in good faith in the reasonable expectation that present arrangements would broadly continue – should be overturned, in pursuit of some theoretical or academic dogma.

The theoretical dogma was presumably Labour's tradition of democratic socialism. But is it purely academic to point out (as many Labour Party members did) that mortgage tax relief is an open-ended, highly regressive and wasteful subsidy which inflates house prices and distorts the housing market? And that the political price which Labour has had to pay for the government's unwillingness to reduce the financial advantages of home-ownership has been that council housing has been left almost defenceless against the Conservatives' determination to sell it off?

The labour movement as a whole has yet to recognize just how far tax allowances erode the tax base at the expense of ordinary people to create a private welfare system which discriminates in favour of the rich and relegates the welfare state to second-class status. While Mrs Castle was taking on the medical establishment over pay-beds in the cause of a universal health service, she was presiding over the enactment of a pension scheme which wholly undermined the universal spirit of Labour's approach to social security. The new pension scheme represented a political settlement with the private insurance societies on terms loaded in their favour. It is a licence for class advantage at the taxpayers' expense which, through tax reliefs, makes private pensions cheaper and more rewarding than the new earnings-related state pension. And as we have seen, the resources for the enhanced private pensions reinforce the power of the City establishment. Funded private pension schemes are less flexible than the pay-as-you-go state scheme. We are now in danger of being committed to subsidizing private pensions over a lifespan of sixty years or more on terms where, if investments finally fail, the state will have to bail them out. The Castle pension scheme has been widely praised as one of the major achievements of the last Labour Government. Mrs Castle proclaimed in 1974 that one of its objectives was 'to take pensions out of politics'. Her scheme is certainly acceptable to Conservatives. The new government has shown its willingness to dismantle the welfare state and to subsidize private welfare still further. But it has left the pension scheme alone.

Private pensions, and the whole apparatus of company welfare of which they are part, must be taken back into political debate. The role of tax allowances and reliefs in reinforcing inequality must be recognized. If we ever want a just society, we must roll back the frontiers of private welfare.

5 The law for the poor

In theory the labour movement has always wanted the welfare state to be universal, providing income and services on the basis of need to all citizens, regardless of their ability to pay. In practice this socialist ideal has always been compromised by assertions of the continuing right of the better-off to their own private schemes of welfare. And in the background there has always lurked the spectre of the poor law – the traditional instrument of controlled deprivation which, however its forms have changed, is still an important ingredient of our society today.

Labour's reforming efforts since the war have concentrated on four main areas – social security, health, housing and education. If the noble vision of the founders of the welfare state had been carried through, our society would by now have been rid of mass poverty and have given the great majority of people at least an opportunity to compete for privileges of income and managerial responsibility. But we shall see that the welfare state fell far short of the visions which inspired its creation and that it has degenerated into a system which perpetuates poverty in the very act of partially relieving it.

The erosion of social security
Until the 1970s full employment allowed the great majority of workers – including married women – to keep a steady wage packet between themselves and hardship. But by now growing mass unemployment is demonstrating more widely what one person in ten already knew, that national insurance, at the heart of the welfare state, offers inadequate protection even in the crises, like unemployment or sickness, which it is supposed to meet; in entirely normal circumstances like parenthood with small children; as well as in cases, like single parenthood or con-

genital disability, which it never tried to cover. The coverage of national insurance is poor and getting worse. Only a third of the unemployed receive unemployment benefit. National insurance benefits have anyway rarely been generous enough to keep the people who receive them out of subsistence poverty. The result is that millions of people have been forced on to means-tested supplementary benefit. The Labour Government in 1948 assumed that this ultimate safety net (then named national assistance) would wither away as national insurance gradually improved and extended to cover the whole community. In 1948 just over two million people depended on national assistance. But by 1979 – when Labour had been in power for half the postwar period – twice as many depended, wholly or partly, on supplementary benefit and at least another 1.5 million were poor enough to qualify for supplementary benefit but failed, through pride or ignorance, to apply. Another 60,000 poor families in work drew family income supplement and several hundred thousand relied on rent and rate rebates. Nearly 90,000 households could not afford their electricity bills and had been cut off, and over 31,000 homes were deprived of their gas supply. Altogether one quarter of the total population of Britain was living under, or only marginally above, the state's poverty line. This deserves to be described as 'mass' poverty.

Much of what is wrong with social security today had its roots in the proposals of the 1942 Beveridge Report which the postwar Labour Government largely enacted. Though it was popularly supposed that Beveridge's comprehensive social security scheme would give cover to all, including people who had not been able to obtain or afford private insurance before the war, it was not in fact a universal scheme for the whole population. For Beveridge recommended that national insurance should stick to a traditional contributory base. People's entitlement to benefits for unemployment, sickness, invalidity, widowhood and old age were therefore tied to employment. National insurance only recognized accidents at work and industrial diseases: any other disability or long-term sickness was excluded. Non-working wives derived their security entirely from the status of being a worker's dependant, not in their own right. They lost their entitlement to insurance if they were separated or divorced from their husbands. There was no cover at all for single mothers. One-parent families have in practice had to rely heavily on the supplementary benefit scheme as the courts have been unable to enforce adequate maintenance from husbands and fathers, while the lack of facilities for day care of young children has made it difficult for them to earn money by going out to work. Even though it was the government's intention to cover 'bad risks', the contribution principle has meant that people who work irregularly – through ill-health, perhaps, or family responsibilities – are effectively disqualified from benefit.

In Beveridge's original scheme, benefits were at least to continue 'as long as the need lasts'. (In the 1930s it was the six-month limit to unemployment benefit which had pitched so many thousands of unemployed workers on to the poor law rolls.) But after a huge row in cabinet, the postwar Labour Government restricted unemployment benefit to between thirty-six and sixty-two weeks, depending on a worker's contribution record – though, up to 1951, benefit was renewable for periods of six months on appeal to a local tribunal. The significance of this retreat from Beveridge became clearer with the increase in long-term unemployment in the 1970s. Unemployed people are forced on to supplementary benefit. Worse still, those who have been unemployed for over a year receive lower, so-called 'short-term', rates of supplementary benefit. Social security officials tried to persuade the last Labour Government to put the long-term unemployed on higher long-term rates of supplementary benefit, which are designed to ease the hardship of living indefinitely at subsistence level. Fearful of being seen to assist 'scroungers', the Labour cabinet refused, choosing to leave the long-term unemployed in acute hardship.

The 1945 Government's most disastrous decision lay in

its failure to fix benefits at the 'decent' level of subsistence which Beveridge had recommended. Since the beginning basic national insurance benefits have remained below the official poverty line. Additionally, Beveridge had envisaged a 'double redistribution'; generous family allowances would be paid for all but the first children in every family. Not only would this help the low paid; it also meant that fewer families would have to depend on national assistance in adversity. The wartime government introduced family allowance in 1944 at only two thirds of Beveridge's rates, and Beveridge had underestimated the cost of maintaining children. Even so the postwar Labour Government failed to raise family allowances at all during its six years in office. So began Britain's shameful neglect of families.

Labour came into government in 1964 with the intention of recasting social security to provide a minimum income for all. But in the event the government managed only to add an earnings-related extra to unemployment and sickness benefits. One of their arguments for this change was the falsely universalist plea that they were extending, to all, benefits which many employers already gave their employees. The government tried to humanize the national assistance scheme in 1966 by giving it a new name and a new ethos. But that has proved to be a blind alley. The spirit of the poor law proves remarkably resistant to good intentions. The scheme is often harshly applied, especially in the case of claimants who arouse the suspicions of officials or who are regarded as 'undeserving'. The Heath Government's answer to the inadequacies of national insurance was to introduce further means-tested benefits like the family income supplement and rent rebates. In the mid 1970s, the Labour Party committed itself to abolishing means-tested benefits, but the Labour Government did little to achieve this. The present government's bleak and punitive recasting of social security has made it's poor law element even harsher.

The Callaghan Government did introduce one significant universal benefit – child benefit formed from a merger of family allowances and child tax allowances. Child benefit is payable for all children. It represents a redistribution in family income from husband to wife, and offers a base for a sane family policy. At first, Callaghan and Denis Healey, the Chancellor, ingloriously tried to escape from their commitment to introduce child benefit fully in 1977 through a subterfuge which was exposed by a leak of cabinet papers to *New Society* magazine. A special TUC–Labour working party was set up to rescue the scheme. But child benefit is not paid at a rate which reflects the costs of bringing up children. The last Labour Government also provided extra child benefit for one-parent families and a handful of benefits for disabled people. But these measures fell far short of the comprehensive benefits which these two large groups of disadvantaged people need to give them the security of an income above bare subsistence.

Free health care for all

The national health service – with it aspiration to make free health care equally available to all – was Labour's most popular achievement. In the first year, 187 million prescriptions were written out, 8.5 million people received dental treatment and over 5 million people received spectacles. Between 1949 and 1975, the expectation of life rose from 66.3 to 69.1 years for a man, and from 71 to 75.3 years for a woman. The death rate among newly born children was cut by half, and diseases like tuberculosis, polio and diptheria have almost been forgotten.

But inequalities in health have remained, and seem to be growing. In the late 1970s unskilled workers were twice as likely to die between the ages of fifteen and sixty-four as professional workers, five times more likely to die from bronchitis and three times more likely to die from lung or stomach cancer. Working-class women were twice as likely as middle-class women to suffer maternal deaths, and their children were twice as likely to die at birth or in the first year of life. Britain's record on infant mortality has lagged behind that of other West European countries. The Court Report in 1976 found that 'children still die in our lifetimes of nineteenth-century reasons'. Working-class men and women were also more likely than their middle-class counterparts to suffer from respiratory or infectious diseases, trouble with their nervous, circulatory and digestive systems, and other illnesses.

It has been calculated that the higher professional classes get up to forty-per-cent more health service expenditure than working-class men and women when they fall ill. While the death rates of most age groups of men and women from the semi-skilled and unskilled population scarcely changed between the early 1950s and 1970s, those of non-manual – and especially professional and managerial – classes substantially diminished. Aneurin Bevan, the architect of the NHS, once expressed the hope that, in illness, 'poverty should not be a disability' nor 'wealth an advantage'. That hope has not been realized.

By 1979 the NHS itself was in crisis. It has always been underfinanced. No new hospital was built between 1948 and 1955, and only one in four of our hospitals have been built since then. Most date from before 1914. Bevan's original scheme envisaged local health centres to re-invigorate general practice, but hardly any have been built. After 1976, the health service budget was cut and was redistributed in an exercise supposed to direct resources towards areas of need. But the redistribution relied on out-of-date mortality figures, not incidence of sickness, disease and social deprivation, and its fairness was further frustrated by the power of consultants and teaching hospitals. Deprived areas like Liverpool and East London were the first victims. Plans for new hospitals were postponed under the Labour Government, and some new hospitals could not open because they lacked funds for their running costs. Moreover, finance for the health service has been directed far more strongly towards hospitals than to the community and preventive health services which would begin to correct the health inequalities which persist. General practice in some city areas began to break down, and community health services for the elderly, mentally ill and mentally handicapped have been shockingly neglected.

Housing

At the end of the war, the private market dominated housing: over half of Britain's households rented from a private landlord and another quarter were owner occupiers. There was no attempt to develop a universal policy for housing like that for national insurance. But Bevan, who was responsible for housing as well as health, began an ambitious housebuilding programme through local authorities and severely restricted building for sale. He put quality before quantity. 'While we shall be judged for a year or two by the number of houses we build,' he explained, 'we shall be judged in ten years' time by the type of houses we build.' By 1979 one third of the population lived in housing provided by councils, new towns and housing associations. Britain was one of the best-housed nations in the world. Rented public housing had broken the link between low incomes and bad housing conditions which existed in prewar days and which persists more generally in other industrialized nations.

But public housing has come under ideological siege. Harold Macmillan in the 1950s broke from Bevan's insistence on high standards. Thereafter cost controls, industrialized building techniques and the fashion for high-rise blocks lowered standards and created unpopular estates. Encouraged by Labour and Conservative governments alike, councils broke up communities by destroying whole areas of housing and rehoused them in large-scale developments where communal facilities are scandalously underprovided. Lack of funds also forced many councils to neglect prewar estates, which have degenerated into modern slums.

Overall, the opportunity to relate standards in council housing to those in owner occupation has been missed. The freedom of council tenants in their own homes has been needlessly restricted by council officials. Very few have been given any say at all in how their estates and environment are run and maintained. Even the advantages of renting over owning – for example, that someone else is responsible for repairs – have gradually been undermined as councils have failed to keep up a prompt service.

The most obvious strengths of public housing have been put in doubt. Council housing is financed from loans which are repaid over sixty years. Over its lifetime, council housing is financially self-sufficient. Indeed, the rents paid for older houses don't simply pay off the loans but also help to fund interest charges on new housing and hold down the rents. Our council housing stock offers the prospect of cheap homes until the end of the century and thereafter.

In the 1970s, however, the rise in inflation pushed up interest rates and swelled the size of public housing subsidies. This was a temporary phenomenon only, as the government's green paper on housing in 1977 pointed out. In real terms, more was being repaid earlier and less would have to be repaid later. In the long run inflation would have reduced loan costs. However, the *Observer*, *Financial Times* and the BBC's *Panorama* programme led a hysterical media campaign against the 'runaway' costs of council housing. Council tenants, it was misleadingly argued, were not paying 'economic' rents for their homes, though in reality they were doing that and more. The media would have done better to express concern about the growing cost to the Exchequer of owner occupation. True, the financial debt on council housing doubled in money terms over the eight years to 1978, but this debt only increases at all when fresh investment takes place. By contrast the debt on owner-occupied housing trebled over the same period – and this increases every time an owner moves and takes out a new mortgage. It goes on increasing even if not a single new house is built. The mortgage debt, too, is subsidized through tax relief. However, in the political language of our times, council tenants were being 'feather-bedded' while owner occupiers were 'standing on their own feet'.

Wartime requisitioning drove inroads into the privately rented market. But instead of taking privately rented housing into public ownership, postwar Labour governments relied on rent controls to protect tenants. They encouraged redevelopment to deal with the most neglected properties. This gradualist approach left many of the poorest and most vulnerable people in our society in the least secure and worst housing conditions, victims of unscrupulous landlords who often evade controls and charge high rents.

By 1974, when Labour officially adopted a policy of encouraging local authorities to buy up private-rented housing, it was too late. Owner occupation, with its attendant tax advantages, had swallowed up most decent private houses and the Conservatives were campaigning to feed the continuing demand for owner occupation by selling off council houses. In any event, Labour's radical initiative was short-lived. After 1976, the government cut back public investment in housing by forty per cent – at a time when one in seven households still lived in poor and substandard housing. By 1979 over a million families were on council house waiting lists and thousands of families were officially recognized as homeless.

Equality of opportunity?

Equality of educational opportunity has been perhaps Labour's central objective. But evidence from both government and independent sources over the lifetime of the welfare state has shown time and time again that this objective has failed. In 1968, for example, the government's *Half Our Futures* report showed that nearly half the working-class children of high ability left school early, and that upper-middle-class children of similar ability were twice as likely to stay on after the age of sixteen. Middle-class children have also taken most advantage of the postwar expansion in university education. In 1979, university admissions figures revealed that over a fifth of candidates who applied for and won university places came from professional backgrounds, though they made up only five per cent of young people in the appropriate age group; and though young people from skilled manual working-class families made up forty per cent of this age group, they represented only sixteen per cent of those who went on to university. But perhaps the statistic which reveals most plainly the enduring disadvantages of class and sex which are built into British society is that only 0.01 per cent of young women from unskilled working-class homes went to university.

The postwar Labour Government inherited Butler's 1944 Education Act which had established free secondary education for all. But it was not to be equal secondary education. The notorious 'eleven-plus' examination was used to separate children into grammar schools and secondary moderns – or, in other words, into first- and second-class education. Only one in four were offered grammar school places, and the majority of children were consigned to schools which generally demanded far less of them than they could give. By the 1970s nearly sixty per cent of children in maintained grammar schools, and seventy-five per cent of those in the state-aided selective 'direct grant' schools, came from middle-class backgrounds.

Labour councils pioneered comprehensive schools, in which children of all abilities would be educated together, and in 1965 the Labour Government made comprehensive education its official policy. But it was very much a *laissez-faire* policy. No date was set by which the change-over from a two-class system should be completed. The government rarely provided additional resources to fund comprehensive schemes and failed even to equalize the resources going to grammar and other secondary schools. Finally, in 1976, the Labour Government did pass an ineffective Act which merely required local authorities to prepare plans.

In 1977, Department of Education figures showed that eighty per cent of state secondary school children were being educated in comprehensives (this proportion falls to sixty-nine per cent if children in fee-paying schools are counted). Fee-paying schools and grammar schools – which too often adopt the values of public schools – have continued to 'cream off' children from the top end of the attainment range. Through the 1960s and 1970s, half of all comprehensive schools were creamed, and some – especially inner-city schools – were losing up to thirty per cent of their most able local children. The media coverage of comprehensive schools has provided a gloomy picture and no one would want to gloss over the difficulties some schools have experienced. Nevertheless, there have been moves towards closing the gap between the schools and parents and the local community. Moreover, comprehensive school leavers getting qualifications have increased from one third to four fifths, and by 1978 over one half of university entrants came from comprehensive schools.

Much remained to be done in 1974 when the last Labour Government was elected: an expansion of nursery education, reform of the examination system with some move towards common assessment, an overhaul of education and training opportunities for sixteen- to nineteen-year-olds, the need for a national scheme of cash grants for young people from poorer homes who wanted to stay on at school, the continuing privileges of the fee-paying schools whose existence undermines the comprehensive ideal. Most of these issues were neglected. Shirley Williams, the Education Secretary, did bring forward a plan for a national scheme for maintenance grants for the over-sixteens who stayed on at school to replace the existing patchwork of miserable means-tested local schemes. An all-party select committee back in 1969 had strongly recommended such a scheme. But the cabinet decided that they could not afford it, and she replaced it with an 'experimental' means-tested scheme in four local authority areas, which the incoming Conservative Government at once abandoned. No such caution accompanied the quixotic campaign on which Callaghan and Williams embarked for 'basic literacy and basic numeracy'. Gradually the point of their Great Debate emerged: it was to fit the majority of children more readily into their role as fodder for industry and commerce. Industry was simultaneously pressing trade unions to agree to proposals to devote the last two years in full-time education to training to meet the industrial needs of their future employers. At the same time, real educational issues were neglected, the resources which were necessary to educate children were reduced and a discreet silence was maintained about the continuing privilege of private education for the few. Traditionally, the Labour Party has wanted a broad and generous education which will allow all children to fulfil themselves, not simply a 'basic' education to fit them for an inferior position in society.

Given the increase in social mobility since the war, it might seem that Labour's educational policies have made it easier for working-class children to get on. But the upward movement of qualified working-class people is largely the result of changes in the job market – the expansion of non-manual, intermediate clerical and semi-professional jobs, a large proportion of them in the public sector – rather than the product of educational and social reform. At the same time, the chances of early school-leavers 'getting on in the world' have actually diminished in the postwar years.

The challenge of sexual inequality

Not only has the welfare state failed to meet its own traditional objectives. It has also failed to give women and the black communities the equality and freedom from discrimination which they have properly demanded. Since the war, many more women, and especially more married women, have been going out to work. At the same time, the women's movement has grown into a powerful influence and has articulated a series of demands for equality between the sexes. The last two Labour Governments passed the Equal Pay and Sex Discrimination Acts and introduced new rights to maternity pay and leave in the Employment Protection Act. Their fate shows again the inadequacy of a political strategy which leaves untouched the fundamental structures of society. To determine a right to equal pay under the new laws, women have to show that they are doing the same, or broadly similar, work as male colleagues, or work which is rated equally under a job evaluation scheme. Women's average hourly earnings did increase from 65 per cent of men's earnings in 1970 to 75.5 per cent in 1977, but fell back to 73.8 per cent in 1978. The laws are not likely to have any further impact on the level of women's wages, as too many women are concentrated in low-paid 'women's jobs'. Though the expansion of personal social services has to some extent lifted from women the demanding burden of care of the elderly, disabled and young, day care for the under-fives has been scandalously neglected. In 1976, there were full-time places in council nurseries and registered premises for only 1.6 per cent of the under-five population. Our provision lags far behind that in other West European countries. We have vulnerable 'latch-key' children.

Legislation against discrimination was a vital complement to action on unequal pay, but Labour's 1975 Act has demonstrated how hard it is to prove discrimination and how inadequate is a strategy which depends on the victims taking the legal initiative. The government excluded its own legislation from the scope of the Act. It has officially continued to discriminate against women in social security, taxation, nationality and immigration law. Even in an area in which legislation can work – like maternity pay and leave – employers persuaded the government to provide rights which are greatly inferior to those in many other countries and which depend on a two-year qualifying period with the current employer.

The underlying problems of equality for women in society have not been properly confronted. Women have neither been granted equal access to employment nor the right to income for the demanding tasks that they undertake at home. Many who want to work do not even register for work because the chances of work are too few or because society believes they should be at home. And those whose time is taken up with the care at home of

71

children and disabled and elderly dependants are not entitled to a minimum income for this necessary work. Rights to full employment and to adequate allowances or wages remain to be developed.

The retreat on race
One great tragedy in postwar British politics is the fact that Conservative and Labour governments have, beginning with the 1962 Commonwealth Immigration Act, taken crucial decisions which make the official status of all black or brown people in Britain different from, and inferior to, that of native-born British citizens. The position of Labour's parliamentary leadership was liberal in the early 1960s, and Hugh Gaitskell, then the leader, promised to repeal the 1962 Act. But a Conservative candidate's electoral victory on an avowedly anti-immigrant platform in the traditional Labour seat of Smethwick in the 1964 election made Labour's leadership much more sensitive to the racial prejudice of white British society than they were to the rights and feelings of the black community. Roy Hattersley enunciated the party's formal position in the formula: 'Integration without control is impossible, control without integration is indefensible.' But Labour's record on control has been much stronger than its success with integration. In fact, in seeking to reassure white opinion, the continuous tightening of control has served to confirm racial prejudice and frustrate integration. In 1968 the Labour Government responded to Enoch Powell's alarmist campaign to restrain the immigration of Kenyan Asians by rushing through Parliament in a week an openly racialist Immigration Act which distinguished between British citizens abroad who were 'patrials' (that is, mostly white) and those who were not. Though in 1974, the Labour Government granted an amnesty to illegal immigrants, it was but a single liberal gesture: thereafter, it pursued administrative policies designed to hinder the entry even of legitimate immigrants – and so to keep families apart.

Labour governments have passed well-meaning race

relations and anti-discrimination laws but their impact has been insignificant by comparison with the weight of disadvantage and racial hostility which black people in Britain experience. Black people have tended to work in unskilled and semi-skilled jobs which were difficult to fill because of unsocial hours, unpleasant working conditions and relatively low earnings. In the West Midlands, for example, black workers tend to be found not in the higher-paid motor industry, but in shift work in hot and dirty foundries and forges. It has been Pakistani workers who have manned night shifts in the Lancashire and Yorkshire textile industries. Even in industries in which they have traditionally been employed, blacks have been under-represented at supervisory level, and they are generally under-represented in managerial, clerical and sales jobs. Both manual and non-manual black workers earn less than white workers. There is substantial evidence of widespread discrimination even in recruitment for manual work. Blacks have also been harder hit by unemployment. Between 1973 and 1980 the total number of unemployed workers doubled but the number of black workers on the register increased four times. Black school-leavers are particularly likely to be unemployed. Few legal actions over discrimination win through. Compensation is usually awarded only for injury to the complainant's feelings and rarely exceeds £100. The Commission for Racial Equality can undertake formal investigations into discrimination in employment (and elsewhere), but its inquiries don't reflect the wide degree of discrimination and disadvantage suffered by black and brown people.

Because they have been concentrated at the bottom end of the labour market, blacks have tended to be housed in the worst of Britain's depressed inner-city areas. Their homes are often overcrowded and lack amenities. They have been discriminated against by residential qualifications for council housing and by loan policies of building societies. There is growing evidence of 'indirect' discrimination against blacks in the allocation policies of local councils. Asian families have tended to enter owner occupation, often buying poor inner-city houses on loans at highly disadvantageous terms. West Indians are more likely to be in council housing, but they tend to be concentrated in the poorest prewar estates. Both communities are often blamed for the depressed conditions they have inherited.

Just as their families have been concentrated in the poorest environments, black children have tended to be taught in some of our oldest and least popular schools. In those schools, unexamined cultural assumptions and the racist ideology of the past have created a greater educational disadvantage among black children than among white children from similar backgrounds. Black children are usually taught about white culture and history by white teachers. The attitudes of teachers affect children's performance and teachers seem to have been especially prone to label children of West Indian descent as 'problems' or 'educationally subnormal'. The urgent need to teach English as a second language has been recognized since the early 1960s but there is still an acute shortage both of skilled teachers and the teaching materials they need.

The demolition of the welfare state
The present Conservative Government is ruthlessly demolishing the welfare state and encouraging private welfare. For two years running, they have cut the real value of state benefits – including old age pensions and invalidity benefits for the long-term sick and disabled. They are seeking to push responsibility for sickness benefit on to employers on terms which penalize families and the poor. Public spending cuts, especially those at local council level, are destroying services. Mrs Thatcher's Education Secretary admitted in 1980 that the cuts were endangering educational standards in schools. The housing budget in England has been cut by half. Overall, the cuts reduced public housebuilding in Britain to a trickle. The implied replacement rate for all housing in Britain is now about once every 150 years. Through the 'right to buy', the best

council houses are being sold off into the private market. At the same time, an all-party parliamentary committee has estimated that there will be a shortfall of 400,000 houses by 1983, and families on council housing waiting lists are likely to double to two million. The national health service remains desperately underfinanced. Higher charges are being made for prescriptions and for vital services for the elderly, sick and disabled in the community. The government's grant aid for local councils has not only been cut back heavily but has also, for purely political motives, been shifted away from the depressed inner-city areas where local authority services and investment are desperately needed to more prosperous suburban and county areas. Local councils in inner London and the big cities – most of them under Labour control – have been forced to choose between raising higher rates from their poorer populations or reducing services and making their workers redundant. The government has taken dictatorial powers to impose spending limits on local authorities.

A majority of the British people now realize how important public spending is to them personally – even if they are not yet aware of its importance to the country's prosperity. But during her election campaign, Thatcher successfully convinced a good part of the electorate that the welfare state was undermining people's ability to provide for themselves and wasting the country's money. Her ideological victory was due in part to the Labour leadership's own weakened commitment to the ideals of the welfare state. The welfare state no longer inspired public confidence or sympathy. It was increasingly seen as over-bureaucratic and officious – not humanizing and equitable. As time went on the more prosperous sections of society benefited disproportionately – especially from the expansion of higher education. Labour's reforming strategy depended almost entirely on a bureaucratic institutional approach. The national health service, for example, developed into one of the largest institutions in the country and has always been run by oligarchies composed almost entirely of consultants and administrators. Social security has degenerated into a legalistic and administrative maze with far too much dependence on invidious tests of means. Even services run by local authorities have tended to be remote and unresponsive to grassroots pressures. Council housing has been administered by officials in housing departments, many of whom cling to paternalistic attitudes which developed during the 1930s slum clearance programmes. They have not been sympathetic to the needs of the large and increasingly self-confident communities which council housing now serves. In short, people have had no say over the form or allocation of the benefits and services of the welfare state. The welfare state has not been *ours*. Like the old poor law, it is *theirs*.

6 The state and the people

It is a common fallacy to regard the present manifestations of authoritarianism as something new. The typical liberal reaction to unwarranted government secrecy, or the over-zealous exercise of police powers, or the more blatant expressions of judicial conservatism, is one of shock, horror and surprise. But the most significant aspect of these and similar excesses is that they are as old as authority itself. And in Britain the authority of the state has been unbroken for some 300 years. In that time, every other large industrialized nation has had a major upheaval and the existing regime has been overthrown or radically reformed. In many countries (France, the United States, Italy, the Soviet Union) the new government has claimed to be established as an expression of the popular will. But in Britain government is still carried on in the name of the Crown. Sovereignty lies there, not in the people. Our system is not one of accountability or of social contract; it is one of centralized authority. In this chapter, we shall show how that authority has moved to tighten its control over dissent and potential unrest as the postwar consensus has broken down under the stress of our economic and industrial crisis, and how the Labour movement's very acquiescence in that consensus has weakened its ability to fight back now against the excesses of the state apparatus and to make the security forces and police democratically accountable.

We are fortunate to live in one of the more free societies in the world today. But not only has our freedom been hardly won; it is, and always will be, under constant threat. Moreover it is continuously being oversold. Real though our freedoms are, they are neither as real nor as extensive as our governors would have us believe. And sometimes they look very fragile. To the young black on a 'sus' charge, to a demonstrator in front of the magistrates after a march against the National Front, to an immigrant challenging the legality of his detention, to a homeless squatter, to an innocent man in a police station denied access to lawyer or friend, to a trade unionist on the picket line, even to a journalist seeking to protect his sources of information, the judicial protection of fundamental freedoms – or, as we are encouraged to see them, fundamental rights – looks remarkably thin.

The business of governance

The unbroken tradition of British government has had one important consequence. There has persisted the notion, among those who hold the reins of political power, that government is a specialized profession, from which the people should be excluded as far as possible – unless the need for their involvement has been clearly demonstrated. This does not mean that government is necessarily insensitive. Far from it: politicians and civil servants alike are notoriously sensitive to public opinion, and aware of the need to manipulate it. They may even seek to promote the interests of the people. But at its best, government in Britain has been paternalistic. At its worst, it is highly authoritarian.

This general philosophy of government – that it is a matter for experts – lies behind the strong resistance to any relaxation of the law relating to official secrets. The present law is so all-embracing that all information given by a government employee is a breach of secrecy and a criminal offence which may result in imprisonment, unless the release of the information has been authorized. Anyone who receives that information is similarly in danger of being imprisoned. All of this has nothing to do with spying, against which the law was originally directed in 1911. It is the final sanction of government which aims to control public perception and discussion of issues by the release only of the information selected by the state in the form acceptable to the state. This is what underlies the system of government press and publicity offices. They are supposed to help the public find out what is happening. In reality, their job is to prevent the public making that discovery by controlling information. The last Labour Government entirely failed to break the civil service's resistance to reform. The party manifesto of 1974 promised a law which would 'place the burden on the public authorities to justify withholding information'. All that emerged was a white paper in 1978 which suggested some minor tinkering with the law. Labour's proposals closely resembled the Thatcher administration's honestly entitled Protection of Official Information Bill, which was withdrawn after being engulfed by criticism in late 1979. Nothing more positive emerged in the five and half years of Labour rule. Indeed, the period was marked by the humiliating prosecutions of Aubrey, Berry and Campbell, two journalists and a former soldier who were accused under both the spying and unauthorized disclosure sections of the 1911 Act for the passing on of trivial and out-of-date information about the role of British signals intelligence in intercepting civilian communications.

The law and order consensus

The notion that government is a matter for experts reaches its most public and significant form when it comes to a tightly knit group of sensitive areas – defence, security, law and order, and Northern Ireland. What these policy areas have in common is that they cannot be discussed without raising the ultimate sanctions of force upon which any system of political power relies. As a result, discussion of these issues is officially discouraged. Here, more than in any other area of policy, information is controlled. It is hard to get at. And what is released is more carefully managed than in any other part of the British state. Here, national interest and national secrecy rule. Here, where the state's power is at stake, there is subtle but powerful pressure to enforce and maintain political consensus. So far in our history, the major political parties have never clashed over these issues. They are above 'party politics', and even above politics itself. The Labour Party has spent over fifty years as the official 'loyal' opposition or in government. But in their enthusiasm to demonstrate that they have been fit to govern, Labour politicians have consistently refused to breach the two-party tradition of secrecy and agreement surrounding these issues. Even those former Labour politicians, who now warn the British public about the dangers of the state taking too much power to itself under a future Labour government, have been content to allow the military, police and security forces to make their independence from democratic control increasingly absolute.

The public's awareness of these issues naturally focuses on what is normally labelled 'law and order' since this is the issue most lavishly reported by the media, and is most likely to impinge upon their own lives. Plainly, people are entitled to police protection against crime and violence. But law and order can mean many things. It can encompass a disciplinary and intolerant approach to a whole range of public and private activities, and especially when these activities differ from stereotyped norms. But more specifically, it is concerned with the police's work in criminal investigation and public order, the administration of justice and the penal system. The Labour leadership's adherence to the consensus of law and order in this more specific sense – and especially so far as the workings of the police are concerned – as above politics has left the field clear for those who run the system to take all the important decisions by themselves. They define the political language in which debate about police activity – if they are forced to have one – is conducted. This means that politically the Left has allowed the Right to make the rules – and the running. The labour movement has always concentrated on the development of economic and social policies. Labour has regarded the Home Office – and law and order in the narrow sense – at best as marginal, and at worst as unneedful of change.

This has left the labour movement without a tradition which recognizes or agitates for civil liberties (and this is true, whatever they may claim, of the Right – both those who have moved out of the Labour Party and those who have remained – as it is of the Left). As with immigration, social security 'scrounging' and so many other populist issues, Labour's weakness has allowed the Conservatives to dictate the terms of the consensus. In fact, under both Heath and Thatcher, the Conservatives have tried to claim a monopoly on the 'law and order' consensus. And when, in the late 1970s, Margaret Thatcher was poised to defeat Labour at the polls on a platform which emphasized more disciplinary law and order measures, James Callaghan's response was not to stand up against these demands, but to push a hawkish motion through an un-vigilant Labour Party conference in 1978 to ensure that Labour could not be accused of being soft on crime.

So the Labour movement has been ill-equipped to respond to the tightening of state control, which has accompanied the economic crisis of the late 1970s and early 1980s. Only where traditional labour interests have been at stake – as with restrictions on picketing, for example – has there been much of a fightback, and even that has been divided and ineffective. The same, incidentally, can be said of labour movements in other countries. In France, for example, the Left mounted too little opposition too late to the Giscard Government's repressive law and order legislation of 1980.

Big brother can watch us

Previous economic crises have been accompanied by strict disciplinary laws (during the 1820s and 1930s, for instance). But never before has the state been better informed or equipped to enforce these laws than it is today. The state's capacity to monitor individual citizens and to control their access to goods and services has increased enormously in the postwar period with the development of computers and microelectronic technology. The distribution of the benefits of the welfare state is founded on an unprecedented level of record-keeping by the state, at both local and national level. Taxation, pensions and benefits, and local authority services are based upon information systems which cover almost all of us. Our ability to communicate by telephone, to receive information by television and to move about in a private car is controlled by a state-run agency or licensing system.

Few of us would probably dispute the need for these filing and licensing systems if we looked only at each case on its own. But, as a whole, they come perilously close to providing all the raw material which would be required in the big dossier on which a national identity card system would be based. The police already have free access to driving licence and vehicle ownership records, through the interface of their national computer and the Driver and Vehicle Licensing Centre. Were we ever to have identity cards, there is no limit to the number of other interfaces. But even as things stand, the police control large amounts of information about citizens. The police's own information service is frighteningly wide-ranging. There are, of course, criminal records. But the police collect far more information on people than that. At the local level, criminal 'intelligence' can range from criminal tipoffs to general gossip, and is known to include such details as whether a person lives in a squat. The Lindop Report on data collection said that police information 'may be speculative, suppositional, hearsay and unverified'. Such information is brought together by collators, whose job is to service their colleagues with information. One area has experimentally computerized this chit-chat. Meanwhile, the Special Branch – Britain's political surveillance police – maintains files on over 1.25 million people.

This archipelago of files could be locked together if identity cards were ever introduced. The state would then have acquired, at a stroke, vast powers of information and control over the people. Even without this, things are serious. For no citizen has any right to know what is on any official file nor any right to control the use to which that file is put. Two groups of people in this country already live close to this situation. In Northern Ireland, approximately half the population is filed on the army's computer at Lisburn. This computer contains an astonishing wealth of detail, which is kept up to date by the security forces in the course of the endless round of checks which characterizes life in Northern Ireland. The daily movements of the province's population are more closely monitored than those of any society in Western Europe – and possibly the world. The black community, and Asians in particular, are also subjected to a degree of routine control and identity checks with which whites are unfamiliar. Information is stored on Scotland Yard's own computer. Raids by police and immigration officers on largely black workplaces, lodgings, clubs and other meeting places have become common. Black people are frequently required to produce their passports so that their immigration status can be checked and must often show their passports to get goods and services which are available to white people without said checks. Under the Conservative Government's new citizenship law, black people will be compelled to produce their papers when registering a birth. In 1978, the all-party select committee on race relations proposed unanimously that a system of internal controls on the black community should be enforced to prevent illegal immigration. Aneurin Bevan's words of 1947 seem to have been forgotten:

I believe that the requirement of an internal passport is more objectionable than an external passport, and that citizens ought to be allowed to move about freely without running the risk of being accosted by a policeman or anyone else and asked to produce proof of identity.

The state within the state

Few people would deny that a country like Britain must have the power to take steps to prevent its overthrow by foreign powers. But in Britain today this principle has been pulled and pushed into quite a different shape to legitimize the intolerable activities of the agencies whose job is to prevent that overthrow. It is popularly supposed that MI5, the state's security agency, is a body which catches spies – or, more notoriously, fails to catch spies.

It is nothing of the kind. Its main function is to keep watch on British citizens, and its computer file is believed to hold more than two million entries. In the hands of the security forces, the concept of subversion has become an endlessly spreading stain. In 1963, Lord Denning defined subversives as those who would 'contemplate the overthrow of the government by unlawful means'. This definition falls within the bounds of the criminal law. But if the security services were to carry on their more general task of keeping watch on British citizens, they could not be happy within Lord Denning's bounds. A more relaxed definition of subversion duly followed, announced by Roy Jenkins in 1975.

Labour's Home Secretary said that subversion encompasses activities which 'threaten the safety or wellbeing of the state, and are intended to undermine or overthrow parliamentary democracy by political, industrial or violent means'. Towards the end of the twentieth century, then, Britain has retained a view of subversion which is every bit as wide as the crime of sedition 200 years ago, when Thomas Muir was transported for threatening the 'safety and well-being' of the state by advocating universal suffrage.

This wider view of subversion now sustains a routine surveillance – telephone tapping, the interception of mail, and the like – of legitimate political and trade union activity. From time to time, occasional examples of this spying on, say, Labour ministers and MPs, and on trade union officials, have come to light. MI5 has no official existence. And since it does not exist, no minister has to answer for it in Parliament. The head of MI5 is formally accountable to the Home Secretary, with access to the Prime Minister. In practice, this chain is frequently ignored. Both the Home Secretary and Prime Minister refuse to be answerable to Parliament. Since the war MI5 has shed its responsibilities for security throughout the British colonies, but it is believed to have doubled in size to carry out its duties in Britain. Not much evidence is available about the activities of the security forces, but what emerges, and the manner in which it does so, is not reassuring. Though official secrecy is at its tightest here – even Parliament being denied information of any kind – Chapman Pincher, the *Daily Express* journalist, has been able to make an astonishing series of disclosures and allegations, plainly with the complicity of the security services. He has said, for example, that Harold Wilson was under surveillance; that 'certain' Labour Cabinet Ministers were denied access to intelligence information on the grounds that they were security risks; and that MI5 officers, serving and retired, tried to bring down the last Labour Government in its early days, and made preparations to publicize evidence from their surveillance of Labour MPs, including two cabinet ministers.

Within the police, the Special Branch also carries out routine surveillance of political and trade union activities, and supplies political 'intelligence' to both MI5 and Britain's police chiefs. Each local police force in Britain has its own Special Branch (though a few conceal its existence). Altogether, some 1,600 officers are active in the Special Branch – a fourfold increase over the past twenty years. Activities have vastly increased in scope and intensity because of the availability to the police of computers and all the devices of modern technological surveillance. Some police chiefs believe that these activities will become even more central to the police's work in the future.

The right to demonstrate
Rights of assembly are among the most important and effective citizen's rights in any society. They are what make freedom of speech effective. They allow large numbers of people to 'demonstrate' a common concern. The complicity of the media in the postwar political consensus has made these freedoms increasingly significant. They are generally the only way most people have of publicly expressing their dissent. The police have always been involved in the control of political and social protest. But with the growth of the modern state, there has been an increasing tendency to redefine political protest and social

activities in policing terms. This has led the police to play a more prominent role in what is nowadays called 'public order'. Since 1968, the year in which street demonstrations against the Vietnam war reached their peak, the police have spearheaded an attempt to strip public protest of its legitimacy. And as the organized labour movement has throughout the 1970s been pushed outside the consensus, unionists have found, too, that traditional activities such as picketing have offended against the canons of 'public order'.

The police have been at the forefront of attempts to impose legally binding duties to give advance notice to the authorities of marches and demonstrations – and the present government has taken up the idea in its green paper on possible changes to the 1936 Public Order Act. This drive against demonstrations has not been provoked by fears of violence – though violent incidents are grist to its mill. It rests fundamentally on an opposition to demonstrations as such. The chief constables' own organization has said that the right to demonstrate is 'widely exploited', and argued that even peaceful demonstrations create a general nuisance in everyday life. The police put out highly suspect figures about the costs of policing demonstrations. And on the streets themselves, tactics such as mass 'saturation' policing, the use of specially trained 'riot squads' like the Special Patrol Group, the unnecessary cordoning off of routes, surveillance from the rooftops and from costly and noisy helicopters all help to draw the line between the political process and what the chief constables call 'the normal process of daily life'. So well has this line been drawn that there was a public outcry when a demonstrator, Blair Peach, was killed during a protest against a National Front election meeting in Southall in 1979, even though the inquest failed to explain satisfactorily how he came to die. Ultimately, all repression of the rights of free assembly is undertaken in the cause of preventing violence. The trouble with this notion is not simply that it encourages the state to adopt the kind of tactics we have described and to develop special riot squads. It also encourages the police to take to themselves speculative powers which can be used at an earlier stage in any operation or investigation than their traditional and legally sanctioned powers could be invoked.

The use and abuse of police powers
The increasing use of speculative powers is one of the central issues in the current debate over the police conduct of criminal investigation. There has to be a police force, and it has to have powers to investigate crime. The police must be able to search and detain suspects. But these general principles can never be a justification for the unsupervised, speculative powers which the police have been demanding in recent years – general powers to search, to set up road blocks, to fingerprint, and to detain citizens for prolonged and easily renewable periods – especially when, the police argue, they should be unaccompanied by any strengthening of the already enfeebled system of suspects' rights. Some of these demands are already police practice. In recent years, too, they have revived the 'suspected person' charge under the 1824 Vagrancy Act, and have been given further speculative powers under the 1974 and 1976 Prevention of Terrorism Acts. What these laws have in common is that they allow the state to detain people even though they are not already under suspicion of having committed an offence or actually breaking the law. The main test in the police's mind is too often the kind of person the alleged suspect seems to be. In the case of 'sus', the typical 'suspect' came to be a young black in a shopping area or near parked cars. Under the terrorism law, it still is young Irish people or people sympathetic to Irish republicanism, travelling between the mainland and Ireland. In neither case should there be a cause to detain. In both cases the police conduct raises doubts about the wisdom of giving them general powers of the same kind.

Corruption apart, the way the police use and misuse their powers has caused increasing concern even among Her Majesty's judges. Allegations of police brutality are not uncommon; the powers of arrest, search and seizure are frequently challenged, with suggestions that the spirit and the letter of the Judges' Rules (which are supposed to protect suspected people's rights) are regularly flouted. Allegations of this grow by what they feed on and, because many of them have been substantiated, some accused persons make them falsely in the hope of persuading juries that they have been wronged.

The political influence on justice

The state has also erected practices and powers which introduce political influence into the administration of justice – without any compensating openness or accountability. The position of the state prosecutors in England and Wales – the Attorney General, who is in the government, and the Director of Public Prosecutions – is becoming untenable. In theory, the functions of the minister and that public servant are to be exercised apolitically. But, according to any reasonable meaning of what is political, this is frequently impossible. Both are placed, like it or not, in the eye of those political storms which involve also possible breaches of law. Their decisions to prosecute or not to prosecute are seen as political decisions and a great and growing scepticism surrounds their protestations of neutrality. This scepticism is nourished by the secrecy (only partly inevitable) which surrounds the reasoning behind their decisions. The apparent enthusiasm with which prosecutions are brought against the press (from the mighty *Times* and *Sunday Times* to the lowly *Leveller* and *Peace News*) and the apparent reluctance to prosecute the police unless the evidence is strong against them do not inspire public confidence. It may well be that appearances are deceptive but, if this is to be shown, both the Attorney General and the DPP must operate more openly and be willing to defend their decisions in public.

Even in the crown courts, the intrusion of state manipulation has been on the increase. Two centuries ago, the Crown was unable to secure convictions for political crimes like sedition without recourse to 'pricked' juries of men who could be relied on to be 'well inclined towards their King's and country's service and interest'. But today, also, state trials are heard before 'vetted' juries. The process is conducted by the police, who supply the prosecution with information in their possession on any citizen on the panel from which the jury will be drawn. And, as we have shown, the police have wide-ranging files on a significant proportion of the population – covering not merely criminal records, but general gossip and hard political information. And these files are increasingly made available, not for 'national' security – *our* security as citizens – but for the state's own security purposes. This is a state which trusts its citizens so little that it is storing up more information about them than ever before; which is chipping away at their opportunities to express public dissent; and which is aiming to use its police to intervene against them on ever-diluted pretexts, reviewable in ever more carefully vetted and powerless courts – and all without even a vestige of democratic accountability. We have allowed the British state to remain almost entirely autonomous.

7 Representative government in Britain

In Britain we think we rule ourselves. In this chapter, however, we seek to establish that Britain has not yet developed a representative system of government which is strong, open, responsive and accountable – that is, truly democratic. We examine the nature of formal political power in Britain: by which we mean the authority to make decisions which directly or indirectly create national policy or which are the means of carrying out that policy. That power is popularly supposed to rest primarily in the House of Commons. It is, in fact, exercised primarily by senior ministers and top civil servants. But the senior judiciary and the senior police and army officers are from time to time important participants in the exercise of political power. This ruling group is quite small and, though it seldom presents a corporate image, can act uniformly when the need arises. It is a group from which most MPs are excluded. Indeed, it largely shares a common background and ideology, and thus a sense of common identity and interest, with the top people in the City and big business whom we described in Chapter 3 – the establishment.

We do not, however, subscribe to the view that governments in Britain today must promote, either by choice or necessity, the interests of the opponents of the working class. The power of private capital has great influence over political institutions, but there is no reason to assume that a socialist government would be unable to withstand that influence if it had the political will to do so and the popular support to sustain it. With the advantage of a radical postwar consensus, amply demonstrated by an overwhelming mandate at the general election of 1945, the Attlee Government was able to carry through extensive social reforms and a large-scale nationalization programme. At the end, it was able to take over the steel industry – against the opposition of the civil service, the House of Lords, industry and the steel-owners themselves, who had initially threatened to sabotage the takeover. The experience of the last few years has also taught us not to underestimate the importance of the Prime Minister and the Cabinet in those few areas of major policy which determine the social and economic conditions of the country. But to replace private capitalism, with all its crudities and cruelties, by another society which not only is more equitable, but also enlarges individual freedom requires the truly democratic government we have described above.

The power of government

No argument is needed to demonstrate that the activities of government – central and local government, nationalized industries, and other public bodies – have greatly increased, especially since 1945. But as we have already shown in the first two chapters, British government has over the same period divested itself of its power to carry out its crucial responsibility to plan and control the British economy. Paradoxically, government power over the lives of citizens has grown, while its power to act in their interests has decreased. Moreover, democratic control over the activities of government, which was never strong, has proportionately and absolutely diminished since the war. Only in its scale is this a new development.

A representative assembly like the House of Commons, elected on a party basis with government and opposition supporters facing one another, is not a body ideally constructed for the prevention of governmental authoritarianism. Criticism of the government, if pushed beyond certain limits, is naturally seen, and is meant to be seen, as an attack on the government's policy and so must be resisted by a majority of the House. This is not to say that we advocate, as do Lord Hailsham and others, the writing of a new constitution to ensure that governments (in his view, of the Left) do as little as possible. For the examination of major policy issues, a representative assembly like the House of Commons is as good an institution as any. But, as presently organized, it is not an adequate institution for the control of administrative and legislative powers and procedures, and is almost useless as a body for the protection of the liberty of the individual.

But the weaknesses of the House of Commons *vis-à-vis* the government are deeper and wider than these. The Official Secrets Act, described in Chapter 6, has increasingly been used to keep MPs in the dark about major acts of state. The Act protected Attlee's authorization of the development of the British atomic bomb in the 1940s. Protected by secrecy, Eden was able to make a covert alliance with the French and Israelis against Nasser and prepare for the war for Suez in the 1950s. The Wilson Government concealed official knowledge of the breaking of sanctions against Rhodesia by British-based oil companies in the 1960s, and the Wilson-Callaghan governments kept secret decisions to spend £1,000 million on modernizing Polaris in the 1970s. Indeed, we now know that decisions to develop our nuclear weaponry were taken without the knowledge even of the government. The Act has concealed more – deference and pliability of those charged with the public responsibility for conducting the nation's affairs. Cabinets and Ministers have too often, in the words of the historian Keith Middlemass, simply supplied the 'party element' in government. For years our national economic strategy has been, in effect, a series of bargains struck by the Prime Minister and the Chancellor of the Exchequer, under the guidance of the Treasury, with representatives of the City and industry – and, when their consent is seen to matter, with the trade union leadership. It has been the role of the cabinet and Commons to ratify these bargains.

Simply as a means of extracting information from governments, the powers of the House of Commons as exercised are wholly inadequate. The parliamentary question to be answered on the floor of the House is treated by both sides as no more than a battle of wits. And written answers, except on the simplest factual level, are drafted on the principle that no information should be given to Members of Parliament which could not also be released to the general public. No doubt MPs because of their special status are more likely than members of the public to be given answers to individual complaints affecting individual constituents. But it was the failure of government departments to disclose more than was absolutely necessary, and to seek to cover the faults of colleagues within departments, that led to the institution of the Parliamentary Commissioner for Administration (the Ombudsman) with greater powers of investigation. In a parliamentary system that worked well and in the public interest an Ombudsman would not be necessary. Today the list of subjects which are blocked from parliamentary inquisition is over a hundred items long. On these the government has resolved that it will not answer, and the practice of Commons officials is often not to allow such questions even to reach the order paper.

A proper distinction must be made here. Our constitution works on the fundamental principle that the government, not the House of Commons, governs the country. Policy decisions are for the government, and so, within the powers given to the government by legislation, is the process of administration. The legislative function is different in that Bills may not be translated into Acts of Parliament without the assent of both Houses of Parliament. The government is the initiator of all legislation, except for Private Members' Bills, of which only a handful reach the statute book each session. But the other side of the constitutional coin is that the government, supported as it is by its majority in the Commons, is accountable to Parliament. To the extent that MPs are impeded in their inquiries for information of government intentions, or ministers seek by various devices to avoid telling the truth, the whole truth and nothing but the truth, this accountability is weakened and reduced. Perhaps it should not be surprising but it is remarkable how far the tradition of ministerial evasiveness has been accepted as normal behaviour. All this, of course, has nothing to do with the proper withholding of information which would damage national security if given.

The individual MP is further handicapped by the poor resources which he can command out of his salary and allowances. These enable him only to share a research assistant by joining with other colleagues. And the library staff of the House, excellent though they are in quality, are far too few to be able to cope with more than the most elementary research demands from Members.

There has been one new development of value in recent years. Parliament has set up a more or less comprehensive group of select committees, to inquire into and analyse most of the activities of government departments. The history of select committees since 1945 has not been happy. Even the famous Public Accounts and Estimates committees did little more than draw attention to government activities which they suggested could be more efficiently pursued, with the occasional disclosure of financial misdoings of greater importance. The Expenditure Committee with its subcommittees performed better, and various *ad hoc* select committees since the mid 1960s prepared the way for the more embracing structure set up in 1979. These new select committees have been trying their teeth on various departmental bones and complaining about the absence of meat. Select committees have powers to send for officials and papers, but if departments refuse their demands, they must directly seek the support of the Commons if they wish to force the issue. Several ministers have refused to produce documents or information, or to give a candid explanation of government policies. On the other hand, the government's decision to introduce legislation to amend the notorious 'sus' law under section 6 of the 1824 Vagrancy Act was largely the result of recommendations by the Home Affairs Select Committee in May 1980. As select committees contain a majority of government backbenchers (though they may have an opposition chairman) their recommendations, when unanimous or supported by a large majority, are indicative of general concern. How far they will develop and become strong bodies for bringing pressure on governments, and making ministers more accountable, remains to be seen.

The day-to-day affairs of government departments are private, and many of the steps taken during the course of forming policy are shrouded in unnecessary secrecy. This is even more true of cabinet and cabinet committees.

The very existence of cabinet committees is not admitted by governments, so that it is difficult for those likely to be affected by decisions to lobby committee members. Indeed, one secretary to the cabinet claimed that the great advantage of the secrecy surrounding cabinet committees was that ministerial members could not be 'subjected to pressure'. Once again, as a result, accountability is further diminished, especially as the appointment of the members of cabinet committees is made directly by the Prime Minister, who is thus able to manipulate membership to ensure that the decisions of committees are to his or her liking.

The power of the peerage

The hereditary peerage remains entrenched at the very heart of our supposedly representative system of government. By far the greatest part of the membership of the House of Lords is determined by the accident of birth into the British aristocracy. There is also an appointed element. Life peers, the two Anglican archbishops, two dozen senior bishops of the Church of England and some ten law lords may sit in the House, all of whom have been appointed by the Crown on the advice of the Prime Minister. The Church of England has recently established a special commission of its own to return recommendations on appointments to Downing Street, and legal appointments are made on the recommendation of the Lord Chancellor. Given its composition, the House of Lords is overwhelmingly Conservative in its political complexion, though there are of course Labour peers, both life and hereditary, and peers of other or no political persuasion. The Conservatives are however always able to muster a majority when the occasion demands. A few life peers are women, a few come from working-class backgrounds, and fewer still are black. By the principle of primogeniture in practice the hereditary peers are all male. The bishops must be male and the law lords happen all to be male and, needless to say, none of them is black.

And yet a chamber so constituted, non-elective, unaccountable and grotesquely biased in composition, has powers to initiate and amend legislation. It can block legislation for a year (though convention and statute limit this power to non-money Bills) and this power is transformed into an effective veto towards the end of a Parliament. This power represents a measure of control over the Commons, and it is a control which is not exercised in the public interest, but only in self-interest and those other interests with which their lordships identify: they have lately become something of a rural lobby, for example. The Lords is also the highest judicial authority in the land, though convention demands that only the law lords can exercise their judicial function. Among the law lords, however, are the present Lord Chancellor and past Lord Chancellors, all of whom are raised to such eminence by virtue of their political skills rather than legal judgement. Convention again has it that the Lord Chancellor must sit in the Lords, and not be answerable to the representative chamber. Individual peers, like Lord Carrington, the Foreign Secretary, and the Earl of Gowrie can hold high political office. These are surely remarkable facts. Even more remarkable is how rarely they are remarked upon in the media.

The power of the civil service
The limited, and largely defensive, power over government of the elected House of Commons leaves room for the exercise of effective power by the civil service. Much has been written of the power of senior civil servants. Their great experience, their length of service and the authority they inevitably exert over other more junior members of the service, especially their control over pro-

motion, contrast sharply with ministerial inexperience, short tenure and almost total lack of power to influence the future careers of the official hierarchy. It is in the nature of the structure of the machinery of government that Ministers can hope to do little more than press forward with a few specific, albeit important, policy proposals.

The evidence commissioned by the Fulton Committee on the civil service in 1966–8 demonstrated what was obvious. Of the 2,500 members of the top administrative class, two thirds were recruited from professional and managerial backgrounds. Over half were educated at public or direct grant schools. Nearly two thirds had been to Oxford or Cambridge. Finally, twenty-two per cent were the sons or daughters of civil servants (though such self-recruitment was higher in the upper echelons of industry and commerce). In 1976–7 the Select Committee on Expenditure found that, for the period 1971–5, while just over a fifth of administration trainee applicants were graduates of Oxford or Cambridge, half of those appointed (rising to sixty per cent in 1976) were from one of those two universities. For 1973–5, former independent school applicants constituted a third of the Oxbridge applicants appointed. The select committee found that the Civil Service Commission did not keep statistics to show the relative class of degree of applicants and appointees in terms of the schools attended. They concluded that this demonstrated that the commission was not concerned about possible bias shown by such statistics. It is, of course, argued that the high proportion of Oxford and Cambridge graduates and of those who attended independent schools is evidence only that those universities and schools recruit a high proportion of the most able students. This is somewhat offset by the finding of the select committee of evidence that at Oxford former independent schoolboys obtain on average a poorer class of degree than other graduates. Much more important, these general statistics are most likely to reflect methods of recruitment to the civil service, to which we return below.

Senior civil servants thus share a common class background with the top people we have described in Chapter 3. They share a common ideology too; and so departments like those of Trade, Industry and Agriculture often become almost pressure groups for the private interests whose worlds they are supposed to order in the public good. Increasingly, as we have remarked, those worlds have a cosy, well-paid job waiting for senior civil servants on retirement. These relationships are of additional significance because of the civil service's power-broking role. It is a tradition of British government that many interest groups form close relationships with the relevant civil service departments, and that they therefore have an unseen influence over government policy-making. The civil service must therefore mediate between different interest groups and translate their views to Ministers. A determined Minister can in the end impose his or her policies on an opposed department, if he or she has the backing of the Prime Minister and Cabinet colleagues. But here, too, civil servants can undermine a Minister by selective 'leaks' and by briefing their colleagues in other departments, who in turn brief their Ministers.

Over all departments and Ministers looms the power of the Treasury. It dominates every other department and itself acts almost as a pressure group for top people in the City. The Bank of England, although in theory nationalized, remains largely a City institution (though with a token trade unionist on the board) and provides a formal link between the Treasury and business. The Treasury's ideology is wholly that of private enterprise, and it defends the interests of the business world and its managers fiercely. It was, for example, implacably opposed to removing tax advantages, like mortgage tax relief, from the highest paid while it was preaching the case for a statutory incomes policy and public spending cuts to a Labour Government. Most important of all, it has given consistently bad economic advice to government ever since, in the 1930s, it argued that government could do nothing about rising unemployment and rejected the

Keynesian economic policies which later underpinned Britain's modest postwar prosperity.

The politics of the judiciary

The class structure of the higher judiciary has been often analysed. The analysis shows that between seventy-five and eighty per cent of the judges of the High Court, the Court of Appeal and the House of Lords went to independent schools and to Oxford or Cambridge. The judiciary is overwhelmingly upper middle or upper class in its composition. A written parliamentary answer in 1978 recorded that of seventy-four High Court judges, over three quarters had attended independent schools, and of these forty-one per cent had attended one of the so-called Clarendon schools (Charterhouse, Eton, Harrow, Merchant Taylors, Rugby, St Pauls, Shrewsbury, Westminster, Winchester). But no less important is the professional experience before appointment to the bench. Members of the higher judiciary are recruited from the bar and are unlikely to be appointed to the bench until they have been in practice for twenty-five years or so. They are men (and very occasionally women) whose professional experience has been spent wholly as members of an inn of court in a very closed community. By this we do not mean that they are men or women without experience of the outside world. They have as much understanding as other middle- and upper-class professional people. We mean, however, that their attitude to the political and social problems of our time is shaped and determined by their class, their upbringing and their professional life. There is nothing in the least surprising about the attitudes shown by the higher judiciary to questions of race, trade unionism, minority groups like immigrants or students, police powers, Rent Act protection for private tenants, demonstrations and protests. Their attitude is strongly conservative, respectful of property rights and highly authoritarian. Secure in their jobs, protected from political criticism, persuaded of the rightness of their views, with the whole body of official state power behind their orders, the higher judiciary is much more powerful, within its own sphere, than are politicians or senior civil servants.

Moreover they are, like civil servants, to a large extent a self-appointing group. Effectively the power to appoint lies in the hands of the Lord Chancellor, himself a barrister and a judge, a political minister and member of the cabinet, who presides over the legislative chamber of the House of Lords. With the most senior appointments the Prime Minister may also be concerned, but in practice in recent years they seem always to have followed the advice of the Lord Chancellor. Before the Lord Chancellor appoints a member of the bar to the High Court, he consults some other members of the judiciary, particularly those who preside over the main divisions of the High Court. It is highly improbable that they will recommend the appointment of anyone whose political views or professional demeanour in court they find offensive or distinctly controversial. This does not mean that a Conservative or Labour Lord Chancellor will appoint to the bench only a member of bar believed to hold, respectively, Conservative or Labour opinions. It does mean, however, that it is virtually impossible for a barrister with views which do not fall within the broad central spectrum of those two parties to be appointed.

The organization of the police
The strength of the positions held by the sixty or so chief police officers (which includes the Commissioner and assistant commissioners of the Metropolitan Police and the chief constables outside London) lies in their independence. In London (except for the City) the police authority is the Home Secretary, and the Metropolitan Police are constitutionally under his control. Outside London, there are some forty local police authorities, two thirds of whose members are drawn from local councillors and one third from local magistrates (JPs). Each police authority has the duty to secure the maintenance of an adequate and efficient police force. Subject to the approval of the Home Secretary, the police authority appoints the chief con-

stable and determines the number of persons of each rank in the force. The police authority, with the approval of the Home Secretary, may call on the chief constable to retire in the interests of efficiency. Appointment to the office of assistant chief constable is made by the police authority after consultation with the chief constable and subject to the approval of the Home Secretary.

Every chief constable is required to submit to the police authority (and to the Home Secretary) a general annual report on policing. The police authority may require the chief constable to submit a report on specified matters connected with the policing of the area. If it appears to the chief constable that such a report would contain information which in the public interest ought not to be disclosed or is not needed for the discharge of the functions of the police authority, he may request that authority to refer the requirement for a report to the Home Secretary for his confirmation.

The Home Secretary may require a police authority to call on the chief constable to retire in the interests of efficiency; and may also require a chief constable to submit a report. The Home Secretary also makes regulations which make uniform over the country matters relating to establishments, ranks, personal records, pay and conditions of work. Also Her Majesty's Inspectorate of Constabulary exerts considerable influence to ensure the general efficiency of the local police forces.

For many years the general pattern was for chief constables in the city and borough forces to rise from the ranks, whereas those in the county offices were either appointed from outside the police force altogether or, for a period, were products of Hendon Metropolitan Police College. This college lasted until the outbreak of war in 1939 and was not revived after the war. Instead the National Police College was opened in 1948, not for the purpose of recruiting officer material, but to run series of courses for all ranks. Today no one can be appointed chief constable unless he has served at least two years in some other force in the rank of inspector or above.

Despite the central controls and the involvement of the Home Secretary, as well as the local police authority, in the appointment of the chief constable, the chief constable is in a very strong position with the men of his force. The force is under his 'control and direction'. All appointments and promotions to any rank below that of assistant chief constable are made by him. The policing of the area and the making of policy decisions are his. He decides or has the power of decision on the bringing or not bringing of prosecutions (except for a few of the most important offences, which must be referred to the Director of Public Prosecutions). He decides how strictly to enforce breaches of law in relation, for example, to speeding, shoplifting, homosexuality, obscenity, gambling and so on. Above all, the discipline within the force and therefore the whole attitude of the police within the area are determined by the chief constable and his most senior subordinates.

The limitations on the powers of the local police authority are considerable and occasionally the cause of complaint by members of the authority. From time to time police authorities try to give instructions to chief constables about particular matters and are duly rebuffed and told they have no right to seek to intervene.

Recent events have shown and continue to show that there is considerable corruption within some police forces and that on occasion this has touched senior as well as junior police officers. During the four years and eleven months that Sir Robert Mark was Metropolitan Commissioner, 478 policemen left the force following or in anticipation of criminal or disciplinary proceedings. Only seventy-six of them had been subject to formal proceedings. If senior officers in a force tolerate no corruption and if the discipline of the force is good, then the overriding power of the chief officer and the absence of any effective day-to-day control over him make for greater efficiency and at the same time ensure that crime in the area is minimized. But if the senior officers are weak or not prepared to be strong as well as honest, then the absence of control can be serious indeed. Unfortunately the number of convictions and apparently forced resignations from the police in recent years has been such that it is not possible to assume that the general structure of the service is satisfactory.

The political significance and the accountability of the police lie partly in the fact that major crime is an offence against the state, but even more in the fact that so much of police activity today is concerned, as we saw in Chapter 6, with what is called 'subversion'. Special Branch activities have vastly increased in scope and intensity because of the availability to the police of computers and all the devices of modern technological surveillance. It is all this which makes the relative irresponsibility and non-accountability of the police so dangerous, not only to civil liberties but to the whole structure of political behaviour.

The armed forces and political power

Many foreigners would find it surprising that the senior officers of the armed forces show little wish to become directly involved in the exercise of political power – though they are, no doubt, much concerned on professional grounds that the strength of the armed forces should be preserved, and this reflects their loyalty to the North Atlantic Treaty Organization and their fears of the intentions of the Soviet Union in particular. But the relatively low profile they keep in relation to party politics does not mean that they would remain uninvolved if a real emergency arose or if a political party in power adopted policies which they regarded as dangerous or extreme. It would be ingenuous to suppose their traditional subordination to the government of the day to be a permanent and unalterable feature of our political society. The armed forces are part of the apparatus of the state. In other countries, the attitude of senior officers – even, on occasion, of junior officers – to the activities of political leaders in times of national dissension has been crucial. Nor is it possible to exclude the armed forces wholly from involvement in civil affairs. Long before the last resort they represent the coercive power of the state, at first supplementing but later replacing the power of the police. In the tragedy of Northern Ireland, troops are being used in aid of the civil power and the political implications of their presence were emphasized during the Ulster Workers' Council strike in 1974. The army has developed its counter-subversion activities both in Northern Ireland and on the mainland and a close relationship with the police has grown up. Some important army chiefs believe that counter-subversion will be the army's major role in the future. The security exercised at Heathrow and other airports, as well as the use of the army when particular services are threatened by other strikes – like that of the firemen or of the Glasgow dustmen in 1975. – demonstrates the close involvement of the armed forces in civil affairs. Whether such involvement in any particular case is desirable or not is a matter of political judgement or choice. What is here important is to note its existence and significance.

8 The cause of Labour

The trade unions since the middle of the last century and the Labour Party since the beginning of this century have struggled against the system of class privilege described in the preceding chapters. After the Second World War, when a Labour Government was elected with a large majority and established the new welfare state, it looked as though the historic objective of transforming British society was on the way to being realized. But since then, as we have seen, class privilege has been reasserted, Britain remains divided into not two, but at least three nations, and power remains heavily concentrated in the hands of a few thousand people at the top.

In the thirty years since 1951 the promise of Labour's challenge has not been fulfilled. Despite growing trade union membership, committed support for the labour movement's political objectives has declined. What has gone wrong? Can the labour movement now re-establish itself and make a successful political response to present-day needs?

The first part of this chapter shows that Labour lost much of its traditional support because part of the movement, especially its official representatives and leaders, abandoned a class-based socialist strategy in favour of a compromise with the existing structure of power. Revisionism or, as it came to be known, social democracy deprived Labour of a coherent analysis, drastically weakened its political programme and undermined the credibility of both socialist values and the party itself.

A second fundamental cause of Labour's loss of momentum has been the manner in which Labour MPs, ministers and trade union leaders exercised political and industrial power. In their dealings with top management, in Parliament and in government, Labour's leaders adopted the style of the ruling class. In effect, they joined the corporate state and their participation made the power of the corporate state almost complete. The future of the country could in nearly all important respects be settled by deals made at the top. Democracy was manipulated by Labour leaders, as well as by top businessmen, financiers, civil servants and Conservative politicians. They wanted to confine democracy to the ratification of decisions which they had reached in private deals with one another. In the end the compliance of Labour leaders with corporatism brought them into a head-on clash with the democratic ideals of the labour movement – but not before it had alienated and turned away huge numbers of people whose active support the movement sorely needed.

The second part of this chapter goes on to examine the present bases of potential support for socialism in Britain. Already many who perceive themselves to be excluded from power, or to be victims of discrimination, are beginning to instil a new vitality to the labour movement. Shop stewards, council tenants, pensioners, teachers, workers in the public services and now also women and ethnic minorities have started to see the Labour Party as a possible vehicle for advancing their causes in a common movement. Members of the party have reacted against corporatist leadership and have started to change the party's constitutional structure.

Some MPs in the revisionist tradition, finding their own positions challenged, have split off to form the new Social Democratic Party. The test for the labour movement now is whether it can unify itself as an active alliance of the working class, the dissident middle class, women and the ethnic minorities to sweep aside the conservative appeal of the Social Democrats and provide a socialist alternative to the politics of the present Conservative Government and class power in Britain.

The loss of working-class support

The Labour Party's optimism in its early years rested on the assumption that in the end virtually all working people – the large majority of the population – would come to vote for their own party. From the start Labour's support at the polls grew dramatically. The Liberals were soon displaced. There was a setback in the extraordinary circumstances of 1931 when the Labour Prime Minister joined the other side but in 1935 Labour's support recovered and continued to rise until 1951. Although, ironically, Labour lost the 1951 election, the party's vote in that election was the highest ever achieved by a single party – just short of fourteen million, or forty per cent of all those entitled to vote. The party's individual membership in 1951 had reached about one million and its affiliated membership through trade unions and cooperative societies was five million. In the next thirty years, Labour's support fell as steadily (apart from an upsurge in 1966) as it rose in the first thirty years. The trend has been masked by fluctuations in support for Conservatives and Liberals. Those two parties twice split the non-Labour vote, and Labour was twice able to win control of government. But, by 1979, only twenty-eight per cent of those entitled to vote came out to cast their votes for Labour. The Conservatives have once done worse than this (in October 1974 they received the votes of only twenty-six per cent of the electorate) but managed a substantial recovery in 1979.

Underlying the loss of votes was a decline in committed support for Labour's politics and policies and a withering of Labour's roots in working-class communities. Trade union branches no longer bothered to affiliate to local parties. Fewer Labour supporters believed in extending nationalization, or in spending more on social services, or even in retaining close ties with the unions. The Social Democrats and their academic allies used such opinion poll findings to argue that the party's Left wing was moving further away from the party's supporters. Looked at more closely, the poll data suggest an alternative picture: support for more nationalization among Labour sympathizers did fall between 1964 and 1970, and from 1974–9, but it had picked up noticeably up to 1974 after Labour's leadership swung behind the party's aggressive industrial

107

policy with its emphasis on public ownership. Perhaps the unsurprising lesson really is that Labour supporters respond to what the party is telling them.

Experience of Labour's leadership in government has continued, on the other hand, to erode traditional support. At the 1979 election only half of the trade union members who bothered to vote gave their votes to Labour. Broadly, Labour's traditional support has fallen as awareness of class has declined. A considerable number of working-class people and a clear majority of the middle class give their political allegiance to the existing system of government and management in Britain. These people are not dedicated to repression of the working class nor are they necessarily antagonistic to socialist values. But they support the pervasive conservative culture of our society and thereby, often unwittingly, provide the mainstay of the traditional ruling class.

Of course this is not the whole picture. The Conservatives also suffered a long-term loss of committed support. Very many people think that big business has too much power. Support for public spending on schools and the health service is stronger than ever.

Labour's socialism
Labour's rise in the prewar and early postwar years was based on a philosophy and strategy very different from that espoused by its leaders in the past two decades. Originally, the party was class-based. By 1918, its declared task had become to represent a fundamental transformation of society. The operation of the market gave us boom and slump, exploitation of working people, inequality of wealth and power – the class system. This analysis, international in its scope, was the basis for links with socialists in other countries. Common ownership, democratically organized, combined with democratic planning, were proposed both as solutions and as polar opposites to capitalist society. The party's political strategy was democratic. From the outset the aim was to win

the power to govern the country by fielding candidates at elections. The party's internal procedures were founded on the same vision. Labour's annual conference, where representatives of all parts of the movement met, was seen as the author of policy. Labour MPs in Parliament would be the party's instrument.

The vision of a transformation of society through democracy carried with it an ethical appeal. The class society which disfigured life in Britain was to be replaced by a different kind of society, cooperative rather than competitive, with fellowship between equals as the principle of human relationships. This required a long-term programme. The party's manifesto could neither be a blueprint for instant and total change nor a list of merely ameliorative items. It had to put forward measures aimed at changing society purposefully to create, step by step, the socialist commonwealth. The party's steadfast democratic socialist aims separated it clearly from both revolutionary insurrectionists on the Left and from Liberals to the Right.

Although these principles informed the decisions and speeches of the party and its representatives, particularly in the period of the 'socialist generation' after 1918, it would be wrong to assume that they were unchallenged principles guiding all party members. The inheritance of a Liberal tradition in the early years, the caution of trade unions and the lack of confidence felt by many Labour leaders, especially when they formed minority governments, combined to dilute the political expression of the party's philosophy. Indeed, leaders often failed to hold to that philosophy; tactical decisions were often inconsistent with it; and individual members and branches varied widely in the extent to which they adhered to it. All this is natural in a large, democratic party. The main message still got across. Britain was a society divided into two distinct classes. In the conflict between classes, Labour represented 'workers by hand and by brain'. The Conservatives represented the property-owning class. This vision unified the party and, as we have seen, brought rising membership and votes up to 1951.

The revisionist theory

In the early 1950s the Labour Party's traditional philosophy was challenged from within. Strategic thinkers, known at the time as 'revisionists' and grouped around Hugh Gaitskell, offered a different theory of socialism and argued for a change in the party's electoral thrust. The new strategy was adopted by the majority of Labour MPs, and Gaitskell became the party leader. But the strategy was never accepted by the party as a whole. For thirty years it caused conflict between leaders and the wider movement, divided opinion, blurred the party's message and alienated supporters.

In essence, the revisionists believed they had found a formula, unknown to prewar generations of socialists, which would permit government to maintain full employment and provide prosperity for all classes in society without the need for any major change in the way the economy was organized. This formula combined high spending, both public and private, with moderation in wage bargaining to keep down inflation. It required the cooperation of businessmen, trade unions and government to keep the economy on the path of economic growth with stable prices and rising productivity. It was, in fact, the Labour leadership's interpretation of the 'Butskellite' consensus we described in Chapter 4. Labour's contribution within this consensus consisted of choosing high public spending and redistributive taxation. According to the revisionists, Labour's old thesis about the workings of capitalism and the need for common ownership no longer had practical relevance. Indeed, the old thesis was positively dangerous because it prejudiced the cooperation needed to make the new scheme work. The revisionists were generally against further nationalization in principle. They stood for the existing distribution of power between government, nationalized industries, multinationals, smaller businesses and trade unions. They believed that the postwar accommodation between the public and private sectors, the 'mixed economy', was a safeguard against any possibility of an authoritarian state.

Tony Crosland, a leading revisionist, restated the main goals in 1971:

First, an exceptionally high priority when considering the claims on our resources for the relief of poverty, distress and social squalor. Secondly, a more equal distribution of wealth. Thirdly, a wider ideal of social equality, involving not only educational reform but generally an improvement in our social capital such that the less well off have access to housing, health and education of a standard comparable at least in the basic decencies to that which the better off can buy for themselves out of their private means. Fourthly, strict control over the environment.

All these goals were to be achieved by a Labour government operating through the institutions of what was, implicitly, a society where class no longer had much importance. Indeed, the revisionists wanted to give Labour a 'classless' appeal. It was consistent with this view, also, that Britain's needs were entirely compatible with the postwar international framework. Labour's internationalism was thus progressively redefined as support for the United States, for an active NATO, for free trade and free movement of capital and, finally, for the EEC.

The Labour Party never officially adopted the revisionist philosophy. But most of its MPs and leaders did. By the early 1960s their principles became increasingly if wrongly identified as those of the party as a whole, so much so that when Harold Wilson as newly elected leader started to quote from party policy documents he was charged with having lurched to the Left. In practice, the Wilson Government of 1964–70, which had seemed to promise a return to socialism, closely followed the revisionist line. In response to economic crisis it adopted the remedies prescribed by Crosland – incomes policy and, after some hesitation, devaluation of the pound. The Labour Government of 1974–9, also faced by economic crisis, again drew back from making a socialist response.

Revisionism had two political consequences. One was

to reduce Labour in the eyes of the electors to little more than an alternative managerial team to the one put up by the Conservatives. The other was to weaken the party by strongly reinforcing the anti-socialist propaganda of the Conservatives and of top people generally and by discouraging potential party members and supporters who saw that the views of the leadership offered them nothing. Revisionism was thus the cause of Labour's long-term loss of vitality and support.

Revisionism put into practice

History has not served the revisionist thesis well. Wilson's 1967 devaluation proved incapable of sustaining full employment and his incomes policy broke down. When Labour took office in 1974, years of underinvestment had left British industry and its workers at a colossal disadvantage in relation to West European, American and Japanese competition. Our industry was slowly collapsing as imports flooded into the country. Membership of the EEC formally limited the government's right to intervene in industry.

In this crisis Labour ministers had to choose between two strategic positions. The labour movement, opposed to membership of the EEC, wanted large-scale intervention in industry to overcome the crisis and maintain full employment. The City and business community supported Britain's membership of the EEC and demanded that Labour's programme of public intervention in industry should be abandoned. Worse still, it soon became clear that unless imports were controlled, the government would have to cut spending to decrease demand at the cost of a large rise in unemployment. The international community and most British industrialists were strongly opposed to import controls, which would interfere with multinational business, depriving management of its prerogative to decide where to invest and where to close down.

This was a real crisis for revisionist MPs and ministers. The claim that they knew how to maintain full employment without making basic changes to the mixed economy had completely broken down. They either had to accept that much of Labour's socialist analysis was valid and prepare to take on the City, big business and their international allies – or else they had to abandon their commitment to full employment and high public spending.

There was little doubt about the choice they would make. Some were strongly committed to the EEC and all were generally in favour of the principles of the western alliance. They were completely unready to make a challenge to the City and big business. As the full extent of their difficulties became apparent they overrode the party's opposition to the EEC and backed continued membership in the 1975 referendum. They totally emasculated Labour's industrial policy and bailed out private industries through subsidies and tax reliefs. They carried trade union leaders with them in imposing a tough 'voluntary' incomes policy. They cut public expenditure time and time again and gave tax concessions to 'middle management'. Finally, in a humiliating deal with the IMF they officially accepted the principle of deciding the government's budget on bankers' criteria, irrespective of the country's social and economic needs.

In power the revisionists left untouched almost all the institutions of class privilege. They legitimized the House of Lords by creating Labour peers. They left open the loopholes in the tax system which made redistribution nominal. They failed to introduce a wealth tax. They allowed public schools to continue to benefit from subsidies and tax reliefs. They consistently reinforced managerial power while relegating industrial democracy to a committee of inquiry.

Conflicts between leaders and the party
The revisionism of many Labour MPs and ministers brought them into escalating conflict with the party as a whole. The organizational ideal that underlies the structure of the Labour Party is that of power pulsing upwards from the mass of the membership. This contrasts with the

way in which Labour leaders have become accustomed to operate in Parliament and government. As we showed in Chapter 7, government in Britain has traditionally been centralized, secret and oligarchical, conforming with the Conservative model of how society should be run. Labour ministers and top trade union officials have, to varying degrees, been drawn into the corporate state and adopted its managerial style. This is perhaps the main reason why the gulf between leaders and the movement at large grew so wide.

Within the party, election of representatives and voting on policies provide the means by which members inform and direct the conduct of the party's affairs. Collective decisions are and must be accepted if the membership, and not a few individuals, are to have ultimate power. This philosophy governs constituency parties, most trade unions and the national party conference. The corporate tradition is broadly the reverse. Power and policy originate from the leadership. Ordinary members of an organization at most provide a check by giving consent or, more rarely, withholding consent – in which case the leadership makes some changes to accommodate legitimate sources of discontent. This is the tradition of the Conservative Party and it is shared in good measure by the new Social Democrats.

The corporate tradition is reflected in private and public industrial management, and even in Parliament. Labour MPs and ministers have failed to introduce their party's different organizational principles into the British system of government. Instead, they have largely accepted those of the Conservatives and the establishment. In the most crucial arena, Labour has thereby been weakened and its purposes undermined. When Labour has been in government, the party leader has assumed the office of Prime Minister. He has then personally chosen those who are to be ministers under him and decided their individual duties. He removed ministers from office or changed their posts whenever he so wished. He laid down the rules governing the conduct of ministers and of government

114

business. He commanded the loyalty of officials by making the top civil service appointments in all departments himself. All MPs brought into government had to sign the Official Secrets Act and had to agree to reveal nothing of their work to their colleagues in Parliament or the party. As we have seen, even the existence and membership of cabinet committees was kept secret so that no one would know who had actually been responsible for particular decisions.

This system of government subordinated Labour ministers to a single individual, the Prime Minister, and it subordinated all Labour MPs to those in government. Backbench MPs, deprived of information about policy choices and of the opportunity to discuss them in advance of decisions, could do little other than consent when, in the presence of Conservative and Liberal MPs, they heard ministerial announcements in the House of Commons. Speeches and questions from Labour MPs usually washed over Labour ministers. They knew that backbench MPs had little idea of what was really happening. Under Labour, as under the Conservatives, the House of Commons generally functioned as an elaborate charade, giving the appearance of exercising democratic power while in reality power lay elsewhere. Constituency Labour parties, having virtually no sanction and even less information than MPs, were obliged in their turn to consent to policies outlined to them at party meetings. They were then expected to advocate the policies at elections.

These hierarchical arrangements often put the Labour Party, with its tradition of accountability, under enormous strain. The most outstanding example of all was perhaps the Labour cabinet's decision in 1975 to recommend, as the government, Britain's continued membership of the EEC. This decision was in opposition not only to the declared policy of the party but almost certainly also to the considered view of the majority of Labour MPs.

It was, however, the assumption of a power of veto, first by Wilson then by Callaghan, which finally provoked the party to assert again its power to decide policy.

In 1973, Labour's programme had included proposals to nationalize twenty-five of the largest 100 companies. As Wilson later described it, he 'issued a statement indicating that the decision was inoperative. It would meet a veto.' Nobody doubted that he had the power to do this, although there was no provision for such a veto in the party's constitution. In 1978, the Labour conference voted for abolition of the House of Lords and the party's executive promised that this would be included in the election manifesto. Before the election in 1979 Callaghan issued a veto – the pledge to abolish the House of Lords was not to be in the manifesto. But although the veto was effective, the matter was this time not allowed to rest. The question of who decides party policy finally came right into the open.

The position of trade unions

Trade unions founded the Labour Party to advance working-class interests through parliamentary democracy. They have consistently recognized the crucial political role of the party. But, particularly since 1940, they have been accorded a place within the corporate state. Their leaders are therefore in an ambiguous position, wanting a vigorous democratic party, but sympathetic to the managerial role of Labour MPs and ministers. Their own access to power also diminished the significance of both the party and Labours MPs in the trade unions' conception of the labour movement's struggle.

The TUC established a general council in 1921 to meet the need for a 'central directing body in future national crises'. The TUC, together with the National Confederation of Employers' Organizations, claimed the right to be consulted by government on labour questions. From the earliest period, this structure was understood at least by some on the trade union side to be a response to the inadequacy of Parliament. As W. Milne Bailey, of the TUC research department, wrote in 1926:

Parliament is essentially a place for rhetoric, for speeches that are going to be reported and will be read by constituents and which are therefore verbose, unrealistic and unbusinesslike. Given the democratic form and method of election of Parliament no reform in procedure will be of much avail in correcting this tendency.

In the late 1920s trade union leaders, influenced by the failure of the general strike, the setback suffered by the Labour Party and the recession, began to establish consultative relationships with employers' organizations and, through membership of government committees, with the National Government. The war brought trade union leaders right into the heart of government. Since then they have come to expect access similar to that enjoyed by top industrialists. Tripartite institutions like the National Economic Development Council became a normal part of the penumbra of government. Consultations between civil servants, trade union leaders and industrial managers have flourished in a world from which, thanks to official secrecy, the elected representatives of the people are largely absent.

Trade unions have on the whole successfully maintained and even enhanced their own power since the war. It is understandable that they should sometimes have been impatient with the Labour Party's difficulties. But they, too, are now in trouble. The failure of revisionism strengthened the Conservative attack on trade unions, and their cooperation is less sought after. They are losing members as their members lose jobs.

Trade unions cannot bargain, even with a Labour government, on equal terms. When they agreed in 1975 to the rough justice of a voluntary incomes policy, their leaders were under the secret threat of a collapse of sterling and a statutory wages policy in reserve. When admitted to the closed world of government, on government's terms, they were all too vulnerable to manipulation. They handed over most of their bargaining power without being able to modify revisionist policies which made high unemployment inevitable. In the end they had to abandon the contract.

117

The corporate state created an environment hostile to trade unions and to labour's interests. Public officials grew disproportionately powerful. Business and City interests enjoyed too easy an access. The democratic element of government was far too weak. Thus ultimately trade unions need a socialist Labour Party if they are to fulfil their own mission. They have to support the democratic base of the party in pursuit of that need.

The Labour Party of the future

The crisis of revisionism has already changed the mould of the Labour Party and has given it a new dynamic. The conflict between revisionist MPs and the party as a whole has come out into the open. Constitutional changes are being made which have begun to shift the balance of power inside the party. Some revisionists have already left to form the Social Democratic Party. Other people, active campaigners at the grassroots level, are joining the party. Overall, membership has risen by 60,000, mostly in the last year.

The party now has the opportunity to draw together traditional and new bases of support and to provide the political means whereby all the oppressed and excluded groups in our society can seek emancipation.

Undeniably during the 1960s and 1970s, women, ethnic minorities, pensioners, council tenants, shop stewards and other 'new' groups of activists placed much more emphasis on their own separate organizations than on banding together to advance their causes by joint political action. Many of their leading figures regarded the Labour Party as irrelevant. This was partly a response to the lamentable record of Labour governments, whose policies bore down hard on those to whom society already offered least. Partly it reflected their perception of the way in which MPs and party leaders manipulated the party. Partly it reflected the failure of the party to recognize new demands that were being made.

The Labour Party of the future must adopt again a class strategy, and accord a full place to the groups of people who most feel themselves oppressed by the shape of post-war society – especially women and the ethnic minorities, and the elderly. These are just as important as the male manual workers and the dissident middle class who have hitherto comprised the main strength of the party.

Allies for Labour?

The struggle for the right to vote brought many women into politics in the early part of this century. Labour women began to organize in 1906 when the Women's Labour League held its first conference and adopted the objectives of securing full rights of citizenship for all women and men – a demand which appeared in some form on Labour candidates' manifestos into the 1920s. Having won the suffrage, women had to wait until the 1970s for any further major advance. Labour's anti-discrimination and equal pay laws have had some impact. But many women feel that Labour's concept of equality of opportunity supposes that men and women can compete on equal terms once reforms have cleared immediate obstacles away. The women's movement argue a more fundamental case. They suggest that men, who occupy virtually all positions of authority, support and reinforce a social system which holds women back and persuades them that they are less capable. This is what makes women accept low pay and a subordinate status at work. It encourages women to derive their estimate of their own worth from men and to compete to please them. Women as wives and mothers are left with almost the whole task of caring for children and the home in exchange for their keep, while men play a full social role outside the home. Women who hold this philosophy naturally seek more radical policies than those now contemplated by the Labour Party. They see, too, that the Labour Party is largely a man's world.

Out of 200 Labour MPs only eleven are women. The shadow cabinet is all-male. The national executive committee of the party has twenty-nine members, of whom seven are women. On the party's twenty-one policy committees, 550 men were coopted last year, but only fifty-six women.

Women have their own structure within the party. Each constituency party may have a women's section which can send a delegate to a national women's conference. The conference is something of a talking shop because the motions it passes have little significance. This structure badly needs strengthening. At the least, the women's conference should be allowed to put its resolutions, as of right, to the full conference of the party. But the key objective must be positive discrimination to redress the balance and enable women to play an equal part in the party's affairs. Local parties should be required to include women in their short lists for the selection of candidates for parliamentary and council elections. The national executive should reserve at least one third of the places on its policy committees for women. Finally, women's representatives in the party, such as the women's section of the national executive committee and the women's advisory committee, should be elected only by women. Only with such changes can the party begin to draw in the increasingly vital and radical women's movement which could do so much to strengthen the party from the base upwards.

Leading members of ethnic minority groups are bitterly critical of the Labour Party. Labour in government has an unhappy record on immigration and police powers of arrest. Today many black people vote Labour only out of fear of the Conservatives. The party has very few black members.

A white party cannot credibly speak for blacks. The Labour Party must aim to enable black people to speak, through it, for themselves. The structure already established for women provides a model. Minority ethnic groups should be able to affiliate to local parties and be allocated places on the management committees of those parties, in the same way as women. The party should hold an annual conference for ethnic minorities and place its resolutions before the full conference. Many years might elapse before such a structure attracted large numbers of black people into the party. But the party would be strengthened from the outset by giving a more effective voice to those who are already members.

A more democratic party

The pressure for changes in the party's constitution which came to a head in the past two years was mainly a reaction to the revisionism of Labour MPs and leaders. Now it must also embrace the need to bring women, blacks and other new pressure groups into an expanding party. This should and must cause major changes in the leadership and in the party's political programme. Changes in the constitution to strengthen internal democracy must be sufficient to enable such changes to work through without too much delay.

Constituency parties have won the right to reconsider their MP or parliamentary candidate once within the lifetime of each Parliament. The plain intention is to secure the right to replace MPs who voted systematically for policies contrary to those adopted by the party conference. The election of the party leader has also been broadened out. There is a demand, on which conference has swung one way and then the other, that the national executive of the party, not a single person, should have the final say on the party's manifesto. All these changes have been the subject of a passionate struggle between constituency parties and MPs. The campaign of the local parties draws its strength from a determination to prevent a repetition of the last Labour Government and to secure a leadership which would genuinely fight for the party's programme.

The essential principle is once again that of reversing the hierarchy of power. More changes are now being sought. Labour councillors are being asked to put policy issues before their local parties. The national executive has introduced the idea of a 'rolling' manifesto, to be discussed by local parties and trade unions and amended at annual party conferences. The discussion of policies is being promoted through a new system of consultation. All these changes provide a greater incentive for people to join the party and to participate in the labour's movement's efforts to change Britain.

The Labour Party is regenerating itself. We have argued that it should organize itself into a wider alliance, but it must be from a class base. As we have demonstrated, class remains a dominant feature of British society. Class can revive as an issue which determines political loyalties.

Michael Steed, a leading election specialist and a Liberal recently observed that if

class as a determinant of political issues and loyalties were to revive, the [Liberal] party would have to fight to keep its place in the political system. If, however, class continues to decline, it will be the two class-based parties which have to fight to defend an ageing electoral base, and the role of the Liberal Party in British politics will expand.

9 The way ahead

The vision of an equal, free and democratic society has inspired many generations of socialists in Britain. In the preceding chapters we have tried to give a realistic portrayal of the pressures, deriving from the international system and the continuing power and privilege of the establishment, which perpetuate inequality, limit freedom and render democracy ineffective. The long-term task is to find a way of overcoming obstacles and sustaining the momentum of transformation of our society in socialist directions.

Most people do not think consciously about this long-term task, however much they desire equality and freedom for themselves and their children. For one thing the problems of politics and the economy are complex and daunting. For another, the pervasive culture of modern society, while generally supporting democracy and equality as abstract ideals, is strongly antagonistic to practical proposals for substantial changes in the existing structure of power and privilege. Such proposals are all too often regarded as being in some way a subversive threat to future prosperity and freedom.

In these circumstances it often seems easier to limit political action to particularly obvious social and economic problems, on a one-by-one basis. But in modern society, which is so extremely interdependent, such 'single issue' politics are entirely inadequate. Many pressure groups are constrained by their need to retain the charitable status which underwrites their financial viability, and are thus forbidden to publicize the political analysis and take the political action which is fundamental to solving the problems they raise. Campaigns against the cuts in public spending are likely to end in frustration, or simply to shift the reductions in spending elsewhere, unless they are linked to a coherent alternative strategy. These initiatives do spark off resistance, provide information, build up experience through struggle; but unless they cohere into a common analysis and cause, they run the risk that problems will multiply and attempts to remedy them will prove increasingly ineffective, and the additional risk that the very ideals of equality and freedom which have in the past been widely supported may themselves be weakened and the possibilities of social advance made more tenuous.

Confidence in social progress has been eroded in Britain, and indeed the West, in the 1970s, and has been replaced by a growing sense of crisis. The only positive aspect of this is that people are being led to question more deeply their assumptions about society. To the extent that a socialist programme can provide feasible remedies to the crisis, it has a chance of attracting more immediate and widespread support. On the other hand, short-term problems may easily be blamed on people's refusal to accept the existing economic system and power structure; indeed, the very ideals of equality and democracy are made the scapegoats for what is going wrong. Equality, it is argued, undermines enterprise, and democracy impedes efficiency; hence the odious proposals which emerge from time to time in our media for a Great Britain Ltd, or to put it another way, government with the political process removed.

Our aim in the remaining chapters of the book is to outline a transformation in the political strategy of the labour movement to lay the foundations for a more prosperous, just and democratic society. But first we must reaffirm the validity and meaning of socialist objectives and, in particular, the kind of equality, freedom and democracy we seek. The other starting point must be the assumption that within our society the will could exist and the means be agreed for a more positive and conscious process of social and institutional change than has been evident in the last two decades.

The meaning of equality

The ideal of equality is nowadays widely accepted only in a limited way. Most people would agree that severe poverty and hardship of the least privileged should be mitigated through some sacrifice on the part of the more prosperous, and many at least also agree that extreme concentrations of personal income, wealth and power should be limited, if only to preserve a tolerable level of social harmony and cohesion.

The ideal of equality with which socialists are concerned is altogether more fundamental than all this because it derives from the belief that all people have equal worth and that human relationships are distorted, exploitative and essentially false unless equality is fully recognized and acted on in practice. Thus the gross inequalities in wealth, income and power which derive from class advantage and inherited privilege in our society must be removed, and the living standards, incomes and environments of the majority of people made much more equal. For example, social benefits and services for retired people must not be regarded as a burden on others, necessary in order to maintain tolerable minimum standards of life for the elderly, but as a natural distribution of the social product to maintain equality between people at different stages of life. The concept of equality between women and men, managers and workers, black and white, healthy and handicapped, should similarly be complete and absolute without any notion of superior merit or entitlement on one side or the other.

Given this view of equality, major redistribution of property, wealth and income, changes in rights and opportunities, and positive discrimination in favour of those who have been disadvantaged must be regarded as desirable and necessary means to give reality to the ideal. There can be no natural right of the more privileged to retain advantages of property and power, however these were acquired.

Democracy and freedom

Freedom is generally understood in contemporary culture in terms of rights of individuals *vis-à-vis* the state. Democracy indicates principally the right to vote in elections to choose the government. Such rights, including freedom of speech and protection against arbitrary arrest, are obviously essential. But they are not enough to achieve a genuinely democratic society. To make a reality of democratic government, people would need to have a real chance individually to influence, and collectively to determine, policy-making at national and local level. This could only come about if the means for participating in politics were widely available, and if in particular access to information and opportunities to communicate through the press and television were opened up. Through their control of the media, top people have privileged political power which makes democracy only partially effective.

From a socialist point of view, freedom and democracy have to be understood in a wide sense. The directions of our society and the conditions of people's lives are shaped not only by government, but by industry, commerce and a whole range of public and private institutions. Full democracy must extend to the policies and decisions of industry and all such institutions. To bring this about there would have to be fundamental changes in their structure; and the political franchise must be extended into industry and business.

Outside government, the main form of democratic influence so far achieved in modern society is the right to withhold consent: in other words, to obstruct managerial and government decisions by protest, demonstration and strikes. This power of obstruction forces policy-makers to try to reconcile interests and minimize strong dissent. But it may also paralyse decision-making or prevent the creative resolution of conflicts. The power of collective bargaining has been largely defensive. Socialists seek a more positive use of this collective strength, and ultimately a more positive form of democracy, based on a transfer of effective power so as to represent fairly all legitimate interests at stake. Our belief is that a just representation of interests can overcome paralysis and release creativity. This view is in fact the opposite of the managerial belief, widespread in our present society, that greater democracy conflicts with efficiency. In reality, the point of democracy is to change the criteria and pressures under which decisions are made. In a democratic system the task of managers is to use their expertise to make choices clear and effective, not to impose their own preferences on others. Democracy conflicts not with efficiency but with managerial privilege.

The perspective we set out in the second half of this book tries to embrace fully and without reserve the objectives of equality and democratic freedom discussed above. This leads inevitably to many proposals for social change which, if they are made specific, seem drastic and extreme in the present-day context. The arguments which sound immediately plausible today are those which fit in broadly with prevailing assumptions and values. The socialist perspective is easily and repeatedly represented as being unrealistic, disruptive, dangerous to our freedoms. It is true that socialism restricts the freedom of the few, but it is to expand and enhance the freedom of the majority. Moreover, the democratic left in this country has a good record of defending and extending our freedoms. The Wilson Government, for example, did much to reduce the state's interference in people's private lives in its reforms of the abortion, divorce and homosexual laws. Democratic socialists have consistently defended civil liberties and fought against authoritarian measures.

Socialism in the Labour Party
The Labour Party and trade union movement provide the main focus for attempts to advance socialism in Britain. But even within this movement many issues, particularly those of government and the economy, are often discussed in the terms in which they are presented on television and in the press. Some assumptions which are widely held obstruct a clear understanding of the prob-

lems of present society, and the difficulties as well as opportunities for socialist advance are obscured. None of us, certainly not the authors of this book, are free from the misunderstandings and obscurities which prevail in society at large. The Labour Party and trade unions are considerably influenced by groups of leaders who have themselves been much affected by the pressures of the existing pattern of government and management. The labour movement, even in its own institutions, is often exposed to anti-socialist ideas. In addition, the labour movement lacks resources. Comparatively few people within it have the opportunity to devote their energies to working out the socialist strategy in any detail. Thus while a huge full-time effort is continuously devoted to justifying and expanding the power of the market, class and bureaucratic institutions in our society, labour socialism remains a subculture. The pervasive view of the world which we see, hear and read in daily life is almost entirely the product of the capitalist system under which we now live. A huge and conscious effort is needed to change our own understanding of this world.

We seek political change which will progressively shift power in the interests of equality and democracy. This process has started, as was argued in Chapter 8, within the labour movement itself. The reforms now in progress in the Labour Party are designed to make leaders and representatives accountable to an active membership which wants a bolder and more socialist programme in response to the British crisis.

Thus the new form of Labour Party which they now seek is one in which Labour MPs, councillors and party officers will respond to the priorities and views of active members of the party, putting forward a socialist case in Parliament, on television and in the newspapers, organizing opposition to the present government on that basis, and planning for a future Labour government to make effective and rapid changes in the political and economic system as a basis for socialist advance. The formal changes to institutionalize a democratic shift within the party have caused an immediate crisis for Labour MPs who do not accept the party's programme – and some have deserted the party – but their broader effect is visibly to shift the leadership as a whole towards a bolder expression of Labour's values and policies.

The structure of trade unions, and pressures from their memberships, are diverse. But the same broad objectives must apply to them – a more systematic accountability of leaders and officers, and a more explicit socialist orientation of their analysis and actions.

The belief that greater democracy within the labour movement would bring with it a consistently socialist stance is strongly contested by many MPs and some trade union leaders. They believe, possibly correctly, that they could secure majority endorsement for their own political stance, promoted through the television and press, provided all members voted in elections, whether or not they were active in Labour Party and trade union affairs. The democracy they envisage is of a non-participatory kind. On the other hand, the form of democracy on which socialists in the labour movement vest their hopes is active and participatory. They envisage members engaging in policy discussions and working through their own ideas with the express intention of contributing to the development of policies within the movement. Our belief is that pressure for socialist change is far more likely to grow and evolve fruitfully through such participatory democracy than if policy-making in the movement is left in the hands of an oligarchy of leaders who are involved from day to day in dealing with existing business and government institutions.

A socialist Britain

How could a more democratic and socialist labour movement advance socialism in our society as a whole? The task at the broadest level must be to raise socialist values and analysis from being a minority sub-culture to being the dominant political and social culture, pervading all institutions, not only government. One important way of pursuing this task is through persuasion and argument, discussing, speaking, writing and campaigning. The formation of coherent socialist views is something to which people could contribute inside and outside the Labour Party and trade unions. There is at present an upsurge of socialist writing and research, appearing in books, pamphlets, periodicals and newspaper articles, which has clearly been prompted by the deepening crisis in Britain and the West. There is an obvious willingness to seek to resolve differences and find a common way forward. We hope for example that proposals we make in this book will convince people in the women's movement that the Labour Party might be an appropriate vehicle for some changes of the kind they seek. A socialist Labour Party might also make common cause with the more radical elements and groups in the ecology movement which have been shifting from a concern with 'soft' issues, such as the protection of wild life and national parks, to 'hard' issues like nuclear energy, transport, the organization of work and the use of technology. The Labour Party could examine the practical implications for future socialist policy-making of the issues the radical ecologists are raising, and at the same time demonstrate how ecological concerns cannot be resolved by free market capitalism.

A second approach to socialist advance is through action and demonstration in the broad range of social and economic institutions. Here, especially, trade unions have a crucial role because of their established strength in industrial bargaining. They can evolve and consolidate pressure for change, bringing this to bear not only on employers, but also on government and even international institutions. The potential range of trade union issues has always been much wider than pay and immediate conditions of employment alone. It can, and to a varying extent does, cover industrial issues, ranging from the operations and plans of companies and government policies affecting them to the pattern of ownership and decision-making. It can go beyond all this to broad issues of economic and social policy as envisaged, for example, in the concept of the social contract.

Moreover it is not only trade unions which can organize socialist pressures and campaigns. In the 1970s the activities of some pressure groups like the Child Poverty Action Group, caught public attention and mobilized nationally on crucial issues. Now, as local government has come under heavy attack through imposed budget cuts and the loss of local autonomy, councils are beginning to act and mobilize opinion in a far more political way than hitherto. And throughout the country, there has been a proliferation of campaigns against the public spending cuts, factory closures and redundancies, increases in council house rents, and the other enforced consequences of Britain's crisis.

The role of government

The aspect of Labour strategy which has always received most attention has been the task of winning elections and operating Labour government. Parliament and government are, of all institutions in our society, the ones which have by far the widest and most legitimate power to institute social change as well as to organize society in the interests of the community as a whole'. We stand four square on the principle of democratic socialism, and the word 'democratic' represents our key condition for achieving our objectives and the key principle of our conduct. Those who seek and use power must do so in a way which can be shown to command the assent of the majority of the people. No minority can justify the seizure of power without that condition, not only because deaths and violence could result, but because such action implies that they are prepared to rule without the consent of the people. This is unacceptable arrogance. It also postpones the process of convincing the people of the benefits of socialist government.

The most immediate opportunity for a Labour government to begin that process lies in making an effective

131

response to Britain's present economic and political crisis. If Labour can argue for and carry out a programme to recover full employment, rebuild industries and restore the welfare state, it can win confidence and support for the longer-term process of social transformation we set out in later chapters. The immediate strategy we describe in Chapter 10 is not in itself inherently or necessarily socialist, but it provides a huge opportunity for Labour socialism to move into a dominant position in British politics. There are two important preconditions for this success. The first is an accountable Labour Party, so that Labour ministers and MPs are committed to work for the party programme instead of using their position in government to oppose it. They could instead use that position – and the access to the media which goes with it – to argue the case for the immediate economic strategy, for more open government, and for a socialist alternative to our present society. Instead of negotiating behind the scenes with interest groups and concealing reverses, they could openly discuss the obstacles to advance and expose the processes of pressure and influence to public scrutiny.

The second precondition is the growth of committed electoral support for Labour's programme to give a Labour government maximum legitimacy in carrying it through. That support would have to be maintained after an election to sustain that government in the face of determined opposition from the establishment at home and overseas. The most immediate opportunity for Labour socialism to win support and to build the credibility of Labour government lies in making an effective response to Britain's economic and political crisis.

10 The immediate response to the crisis

The most pressing issue in British politics today is how the crisis of mass unemployment, inflation, industrial collapse and public spending cuts can be overcome. The labour movement's claim is that a Labour government, which took powers to plan the expansion of the economy and control trade, could secure full employment, reinvigorate industry and restore the welfare state within the lifetime of a Parliament. Labour's policies are often described as the 'alternative economic strategy', and we go on to explain them in detail. The basic proposals can be set out simply:

- *expansion of the economy* to raise output, restore full employment and bring about higher living standards all round;
- *large increases in public spending* to reactivate the economy, provide jobs both directly and indirectly, and to restore public services;
- *exchange controls* to stop the City and international finance from undermining the strategy through a 'flight from sterling' and financial crisis;
- *import controls* to prevent an immediate trade deficit and to allow Britain time to plan its trade in negotiation with the rest of the world;
- *public powers* over the investment policies of the pension funds and other semi-socialized wealth in the hands of the City institutions until such time as they can be taken into common ownership; and
- *industrial regeneration* through expansion of the economy and publicly directed investment; an extension of common ownership of large companies; and compulsory planning agreements, negotiated between the government, large companies and their workers, to bring

about investment, production and employment policies in the public interest.

These proposals are a major challenge to the existing international economic system because they require the government to exercise powers of control over trade, finance and industry which are at present in the hands of the EEC, international banks and multinational companies. At the same time, it is a challenge to the British establishment, who are committed to keeping Britain within the existing framework of the international capitalist order. It also, of course, directly threatens their own interests.

Labour's strategy for developing our economy could be the first step in a long-term and profound change in the whole pattern of our society and its international relationships. The success of this first stage in meeting people's immediate needs for employment, public services and benefits, and higher living standards would demonstrate the practical advantages of Labour's perspective of continuing change. To succeed, the strategy would also have to deal effectively with opposition from those within and outside Britain who are against its development into a self-governing and more equal country. Given the huge obstacles to launching the strategy and making it effective, it is essential to be realistic about what can and what cannot be achieved at the first stage. To begin with, the strategy will largely have to operate through existing institutions. It certainly cannot rely on full implementation of fundamental reforms which would take many years to carry through. The questions we seek to answer in this chapter are therefore specific and narrow. What changes are necessary if a British government is to be able to implement a speedy return to full employment? How can the necessary changes be carried through?

The economics of decline
The claim is that national economic planning can succeed where the present international order patently fails, as we

showed in Chapters 1 and 2. This claim is the basis of the confidence of Labour socialists in opposing not only Mrs Thatcher's policies, which are plunging Britain into hyper-recession, but also the 'consensus' policies advocated by politicians of the centre – the Tory 'wets', Liberals, Social Democrats and Right-wing Labour – which hark back to the failed remedies tried in the 1970s. Before we show how the alternative strategy could be implemented, we must explain how its logic differs from that of Mrs Thatcher's policies and from those of centre politicians.

Mrs Thatcher's aim was to eliminate inflation and restore prosperity by relying on the private enterprise economy. This aim required profound changes in present society. Wages would have to be determined not by any concept of justice but solely with reference to market forces. People would have to rely on whatever they could secure individually in the private market rather than what might be provided collectively. Such changes have been enforced by cutting public spending and seeking to restrict credit to the point at which managers and workers would have no choice but to accept the dictates of the market. Implicitly, since the dominant market forces are nowadays those of the international system, this meant that our economy and society would have to adapt fully to the requirements of the EEC and multinational business. Britain would be entirely at the mercy of anarchic global competition and recession for however long the chaos of the international system persisted.

The consequences of Mrs Thatcher's policies have been incredibly damaging. Cuts in public spending and restriction of credit have not stimulated a more dynamic and competitive private sector. On the contrary, both public and private industries have contracted and investment has fallen. Millions of people have become the luckless victims of unemployment and cuts in social benefits and real wages. The government has engaged in a destructive campaign to make councils close down services and sack workers and to make nationalized industries close plants in a desperate attempt to save money. But in our interdependent economy, money cannot be saved so easily. When industries cut back or close down, their suppliers lose sales and the government loses tax revenue. When workers are made redundant, the government has to pay out more unemployment and supplementary benefit. Money is not saved, but is used to less and less purpose. The terms for converting Britain into a viable private enterprise economy, if this could ever be done, are evidently far tougher than most people realized. The short-term price is bankruptcy, mass unemployment and increasing poverty. In the long term, the whole structure of our economy and society would come to be determined by the international market system with little scope for any independent national choice.

By contrast, Labour's strategy starts from the principle of social justice. Through public enterprise and planning, it aims to subordinate the dictates of private profitability to democratic decisions about the kind of economy and society we wish to live in. Through public benefits and services, it aims to distribute resources far more fairly and equally than can be done by market forces.

Centre politicians denounce the severity of Mrs Thatcher's policies, and express a belief in the need to reconcile social justice and the market system. But they are not willing to contemplate any major change in the way our economy is subject to the rules of the international capitalist market. Throughout the 1970s, the centre politicians who dominated the Heath and later Labour Governments hoped to reconcile membership of the Common Market with prosperity in Britain, and to persuade the City of the needs of industry and the welfare state. The centre's 'consensus' approach failed time and time again. The unwillingness of the last Labour Government to challenge the rules and interests of international finance and big business led inevitably to the collapse of the Labour Party's industrial strategy in 1975 and to the passive acceptance of the deflationary package and public spending cuts imposed in 1976 as the price of an IMF loan. Yet some proponents of the continuing 'consensus' approach –

among them the Social Democrats who have split away from the Labour Party – appear to be ready to accept continued high unemployment and industrial decline as the price to be paid for maintaining the present form of the mixed economy and remaining in the EEC. They talk sadly of the need for 'realism'. But theirs is the realism of despair.

The only firm policy of centre politicians is their insistence on the need for a permanent incomes policy – or, to put it more bluntly, wage control. At its most negative, their purpose is to prevent inflation from undermining the prosperity of the middle and upper class, which is periodically jeopardized by rising prices when trade unions bargain too effectively on behalf of wage earners. Somewhat more positively, some centre politicians argue that wage control, combined with a sharp fall in the pound sterling, would raise the profits of British exporters and help to price imports out of our market. The logic is that Britain could achieve a more dynamic position in world markets and regain employment through a shift from wages to profits. This is a rather theoretical idea. Some improvement in exports has indeed been achieved in Britain and other countries when wage control was combined with devaluation (for example, by the Labour Government in 1967). But the problems of British industry today are out of all proportion to this remedy. Thus, at best, centre policies – including those of the Social Democratic Party – would make Britain's crisis less horrendous than under the present government's suicidal policies, and might slow down our continued decline.

For centre politicians, full employment is a vague and uncertain hope. The certainty is that Britain's membership of the EEC must be preserved and that our society must evolve gradually within that framework. By contrast, Labour's strategy makes full employment its first priority and seeks a new pattern of international relationships, outside the EEC, as the basis for regenerating our economy and society.

The economics of prosperity

Public spending is not simply a way of providing services and benefits that we need. Increases in public spending can also play a vital role in restoring full employment and industrial recovery. This is not an untried proposition. It is a return to the Keynesian policies on which our postwar recovery was founded. Increases in public spending provide jobs directly in schools, hospitals, factories, public transport, nationalized industries and other public services and utilities, and indirectly provide more business and employment for industries of every kind – large-scale manufacturing, construction, transport, shops and services in the high street. Spending on teachers' salaries, higher pensions or building council homes feeds into the rest of the economy as earnings and benefits are spent and building workers and architects are employed. Reactivating the economy through higher public spending will not only provide jobs throughout the economy and raise production, but will also ease financial problems caused by the slump. As sales rise, profits will improve, bankruptcies will be reduced and nationalized industries will come out of the red; tax revenues will grow and the government will no longer have to pay out huge sums (over £2,000 million this year) to maintain a growing army of unemployed people, or to prop up loss-making businesses. The benefit in terms of production and income could be large. With a rise in employment of over ten per cent, and full use of productive resources, Britain's national income could be increased by some twenty to thirty per cent within three or four years. This is equivalent to an additional £2,000 or £3,000 a year for every family in the country. Most of this additional production and income would, however, have to be divided between investment in industry, transport, energy, housing and other kinds of infrastructure and improved public services and benefits. Its investment would have to be planned to match the kind of jobs and production which could be expanded rapidly and to meet the most urgent economic and social needs. There would be some rise in the private incomes of most people who still now have jobs. But the main gains would be invested in reconstruction, higher quality public services of all kinds and higher living standards for people who are now unemployed or suffering from cuts in the welfare state.

The strategy would not work miracles. It would not eliminate inflation, make industries efficient overnight or abolish low-paid boring work. But it would create employment, fund social investment, and open up the way for a longer-term development of our economy through common ownership. It could also provide the base for building a more open and diverse society with a wider range of individual and social choice than we have had in the trap of an unplanned international market.

There are many obstacles to putting this strategy into action. The government will need a strong political will and widespread public understanding and backing for its plans. The main political and institutional problem is how the government could gain sufficient control over finance, trade and the balance of payments – and, in particular, how it could negotiate workable new agreements with the EEC and other international institutions. Several economic problems have to be dealt with. Britain's industrial capacity is inadequate and out of date. Britain depends too heavily on imports not only for raw materials but for many important industrial products. Inflationary pressures, arising from low productivity, low pay and conflicts over the distribution of incomes, have accumulated.

Essential first steps
The immediate obstacle to a Labour government's attempting to restore full employment through high public spending and investment is the virtual certainty of a full-scale financial crisis. The unwillingness of the City and international financiers to underwrite Labour's programme would imply 'loss of confidence' in any government committed to carrying the programme out. Pressure to transfer funds from sterling into other currencies would cause a collapse of the exchange rate. Unwillingness to

lend to the government would cause a collapse of the market for government securities and send interest rates sky-high. Such a crisis of confidence could occur at any time after an election in which a Labour government came to power. It would not only make public spending difficult to finance; it would dramatically escalate the cost of imports of food, raw materials and components on which consumers and industries depend, raise the cost of working capital and threaten spiralling inflation. No government could realistically count on organizing an economic recovery in such circumstances, or even with the threat of such a crisis hanging over it.

The first step which must be undertaken, therefore, from the moment any future Labour government comes into office, is to impose emergency controls on the City and the banking system to block movements of funds out of sterling and fix the exchange rate, to regulate interest rates and to ensure the supply of funds to the government for investment in the public spending increases we need. All investing institutions would have to be prevented from disposing of government securities and moving their money out of the country. Secondly, import controls would be essential to prevent a massive trade deficit once an expansion of spending got going. An emergency general tariff, except for food and raw materials, would deter any pre-emptive rush to bring goods into Britain. The imposition of such controls would amount to a seizure of power over the City and over multinational business. Import tariffs would be illegal under EEC and the articles of GATT. Blocking the movement of funds out of sterling could fall foul of IMF rules. It was the difficulty and magnitude of such an assertion of our independence which led recent Labour cabinets to choose expenditure cuts, high interest rates and incomes policies as, in their view, the lesser evil. This strategy would precipitate an international challenge to the government's legitimacy – a challenge which most of the British establishment would support. There would be immediate negotiations in which foreign governments and international institutions sought to force the Labour government to back down and dismantle the tariffs and financial controls it had imposed.

The essential question is whether and how the government could at that point negotiate arrangements which allowed it to retain sufficient powers to plan finance and foreign trade on a longer-term basis. Without such powers a rapid expansion of public spending could not be sustained, and hopes of achieving full employment would have to be abandoned. The most important factor would be the attitude of the public both in Britain and in the other western countries. The alliance of which Britain is a member is after all one of democracies. Western governments could not threaten direct intervention in Britain's affairs without incalculable political risks. Indeed, the danger of 'retaliation' and pressure for overt economic sanctions against Britain would be tempered by the need to avoid an excessively punitive posture. Most likely, other governments and international institutions would take symbolic action, threatening worse unless the issues were resolved. Therefore, the strength of Britain's position would depend first and foremost on whether the government's actions were widely understood to be necessary and whether they were thought to be significantly damaging to other countries. The labour movement should begin now to argue the case for the strategy much more widely in this country, and to link it with struggles against public spending cuts, redundancies and factory closures. The Labour Party and trade unions should be discussing the proposals with the political Left and labour movements in Western Europe, as part of a common strategy against the recession, spreading unemployment, the power of the multinationals and the chaos of the international capitalist market.

Apart from this, there would be more objective negotiating levers. The economies of Western Europe are now greatly interdependent. So far as other EEC countries are concerned, interdependence is a two-way affair. Some important British industries depend on exports to their markets. They depend on Britain, not only as an export market for their industries, but also as a source of oil from the North Sea and, more important still, as a key partner in their agricultural policy. Without Britain, they would face huge costs in disposing of food surpluses. This is not to say that Britain could get its way on all counts. Rather, once the British government had declared its intention of leaving the EEC in order to pursue independent policies, there would be plenty of scope for a realistic negotiation in which both sides took account of the other's vulnerabilities. It would be important for other EEC members, especially France and West Germany, that Britain recognized their agricultural and energy problems, just as it is important for Britain that they should recognize our crisis of deindustrialization.

Britain's departure from the EEC need not cause a collapse of European unity. It would indicate instead the need for a more diverse pattern of development in Europe than that offered by the EEC's perspective of integration under Treaty of Rome rules. By giving up insistence on uniformity and standardization, the differing needs of all parts of Europe – and not simply of the EEC states – could be brought into the open, and new possibilities of wider relationships would be created. Many people are concerned that we would be 'exporting' unemployment. In fact, planned growth could well be the only way of increasing our trade and, ultimately, importing more rather than fewer goods from abroad.

The United States, the IMF and the world community at large would have their own anxieties about independent policies in Britain. They would worry about the role of the City and sterling in the international financial system, about the impact of the new policies on multinationals and on trade in different parts of the world. All these matters would have to be negotiated. But it is important to grasp that this need not be an all-or-nothing confrontation. Britain is by now in most respects a small and uninfluential country, and power in the rest of the world is diffused. As a country we are neither in the position of imposing our own will nor of being forced to accept the will of others. We are in a bargaining situation where demands can be made and the gain from insistence on some points has to be weighed against the cost of concession on others. So long as we know our own priorities and take account of the interests of other countries, there is no reason why a British government should not negotiate new trading and financial arrangements with European countries and those in other parts of the world.

First stages of planning

Supposing that essential controls on foreign exchange, trade and international finance were in place, the main dynamic of economic expansion, creation of jobs and regeneration of industry in the first years would come from public spending through existing institutions. Local government, ministries, nationalized industries and other public enterprises would have to carry out urgent programmes to get industries on the move, restore public services hit by cuts, improve social benefits and begin new investment in infrastructure of all kinds.

If the programme of higher spending is to be creative and respond to genuine needs it cannot be laid down centrally from Whitehall but must be organized in an open and democratic manner drawing on the widest possible range of ideas and experience. Trade unions would play a crucial role.

The labour movement has already put forward proposals for open government, tripartite planning and devolved decision-making which could form the means for constructive implementation of spending programmes. The central government, apart from organizing the provision of funds, would have to take responsibility for certain specific problems, which we must now consider, in the overall pattern of economic expansion.

Trade and industry

Britain's industrial capacity, after years of decline, has suffered severe damage under the Thatcher Government. By no means all the materials, components and machinery needed for reindustrialization could immediately be produced in Britain. In the short term, higher imports of essential products would help to overcome such bottlenecks and less essential imports would have to be more tightly restricted to make way. At the same time, investment in new production facilities would urgently be needed to prevent worsening shortages as expansion of the economy proceeded. The government would therefore have to coordinate the pattern of imports and investment plans of companies in key sectors of industry.

The planning of trade and industry would also have to meet various specific domestic and external requirements. Within Britain, it must take account of employment problems in badly hit cities and regions. In relation to Europe and the Third World, the pattern of imports would have to take account from the start of particularly crucial needs, including those which came up in negotiations. Britain could not expect to reach a reasonable settlement with the EEC and international institutions unless its new policies gave assurance to other countries on such points. The central government would have to be hard at work adjusting import plans and negotiating investment and exports with key companies, trade unions, foreign governments and international institutions. The aim should be to achieve a clear set of principles and instruments as a basis for such negotiated planning.

Dealing with specific industrial crises
In the context of rising public spending and general economic recovery there would be few of the large redundancies and factory closures which have been daily news in the past two years. But this does not mean that the government would no longer have to deal with industrial conflicts and crises. Apart from continuing difficulties in some declining sectors, companies might well run into conflict with trade unions or the government on general or specific aspects of the new policies. This need not be a question of sabotage. Companies may simply have planned their international operations on the assumption

144

that former policies, and Britain's decline, would continue and face dilemmas as the new situation came into conflict with their pre-existing plans.

The government must have sufficient bargaining power *vis-à-vis* companies, including multinationals, to ensure a decisive change in the direction of the development of industry, and it must be able to link the energy of workers and trade unions into the new process. Conflicts and crises in industry will have to be resolved in accordance with these aims. Sometimes a solution may be found through provision of finance, through the agency of existing public enterprises or through the new instrument of import control. In other cases the government will have to be ready to change the top management or ownership of the enterprise if its existing owners or managers are not ready to follow a new approach. The formation of cooperatives or public enterprises of various forms, with workers' support, will be a valid way of responding to such crises. Indeed, without such a perspective of possible changes in management and ownership the whole process of recovery and reindustrialization might be blocked by conflicts in a few key industries.

Finance and inflation

Traditional 'reflation' of the economy, for example that undertaken by the Heath Government in 1972–3, usually meant pouring out money through government contracts, tax cuts and easy credit, leading to booms in property, speculative building, consumer durables and imports which distorted the whole process of expansion. Such pressures for unbalanced growth could certainly not be afforded in a sustainable recovery from the present slump.

It is evident that credit will have to be provided for investment and for the initial expansion of public spending. Also the exchange rate for sterling will have to be reduced to a level at which industries have a better chance of competing internationally and sustaining their exports.

There are specific actions the government could take to prevent the expansion of credit and the fall in the exchange rate from feeding accelerated inflation. For example, it could regulate the use of credit by placing limits on funds lent by banks and other institutions for low-priority uses. At the same time it could allocate part of the revenue from import tariffs to subsidizing basic items in the cost of living.

Apart from such specific actions, the general impact of the recovery programme on wages, salaries, profits, rents and other incomes would be a crucial political issue. A comprehensive, centrally determined, statutory incomes policy would not accord with the philosophy of democratic freedom we wish to advance. But this does not absolve the government from the need to prevent an inflationary free-for-all. Incomes policies would certainly be necessary, including strategies for profits, pay and taxation as well as selective price controls to prevent profiteering.

The political perspective

The success of an independent, planned recovery of the British economy will depend ultimately on whether it is politically attractive to the great majority of people. Success would give hope for creative development of our own society and would beyond doubt offer an important model to other countries, particularly in Europe, which also are suffering from atrophy of the system under which they have developed since the war.

The best encouragement that a new Labour government could offer in terms of social and political perspectives would be to institute certain immediate reforms, including steps towards industrial democracy, procedures for open government, aid for low-income and disadvantaged groups, and so on. Such action would build and consolidate support and make sure that the new process of development was constructive. The short-term response to Britain's crisis must be related to a longer-term vision of how we want our society to develop. That perspective is discussed in the remaining chapters of this book.

146

11 A strong and open government

The programme of action by a future Labour government, discussed in the preceding chapter, implicitly requires major advances in the system of government if it is to be carried out successfully. For one thing, the Labour government would face a major problem in maintaining and strengthening public confidence against a barrage of criticism from the City, top management, Whitehall and Westminister as well as from international institutions and foreign companies and governments. The programme could not be put into effect unless public support was strong enough to give Labour MPs and ministers effective mastery over the official machinery of government and real bargaining power in their negotiations with domestic and foreign institutions.

Another reason why reform of government would be urgent and indispensable is that the programme, if put into effect, would give the central government much increased powers of control over finance, trade and industry which must be made democratically accountable if they are not to become potential instruments of increased power in the hands of top people.

In the long run the government and Parliament must play a major part in the process of active development of our economy and change in our society. We can entrust such tasks to government only if we are confident that we can make the system of government effectively and permanently democratic. A socialist who is faced with the task of reforming the institutions and practices of capitalism must reconcile two principles. The first is the need for the powers of government to be strong in the face of entrenched private interests. The second is the need to preserve, indeed improve, the means whereby all those in authority can be scrutinized and held to account in public. Socialists must broaden the back of government and strengthen the rod that beats it. Otherwise, even if government achieves many of the ends for which we hope – greater equality and security, a fairer distribution of wealth, a rising standard of living – a price will be paid in loss of liberty.

We envisage a reform of government which will ensure that people know what is really happening, are free to express their own views and, by debate as well as by election, are able to determine the conduct of government nationally, with effective protection against abuse of state power, and to share in government locally. In this chapter, we consider the various areas in which liberty and democracy need to be strengthened. First, we propose important changes in ministerial powers, the civil service and Parliament to make a reality of the principle of elected government. We then turn to the interlinked issues of public access to information and the role of the media in transmitting views and analyses throughout our society. The role of government does not begin and end in Westminster and Whitehall. Democracy and accountability need to be strengthened both in local government and in the conduct of other public services and bodies, and local communities can be more directly involved both in making decisions at local level and in the delivery of services. Finally, we turn to the issue of social control and consider changes in the role of the security services, the police, the law and legal profession, and the courts.

Ministers and the civil service
The civil service machine should never be in a position to dominate, and sometimes frustrate, the policies of elected government. Ministers, who are the representatives of Parliament in government, must have a clear command over the permanent civil service. Yet it would not be practicable simply to replace senior civil servants by ministers and nominees brought into government, since the know-how of civil servants is necessary to the efficient conduct of government.

The main solutions lie in allowing ministers to draw widely on outside advice as well as giving them powers to bring in their own teams of advisers and to have control over the assignment of permanent officials to key posts in their department. Open government would give ministers the chance to test out the facts, analyses and options presented to them by the permanent civil service. Ministers must be free to consult political colleagues, their party, trade unions, businesses, professionals, experts and interested pressure groups in order to form broadly based judgements – and to do so with total cooperation from their officials. They must be able to employ advisers of their own to assist in this process and, initially at least, the need for such extra staff is bound to be substantial. When they lack confidence in a key permanent official, they must be entitled to call for a suitably qualified replacement. The civil service would retain major duties as the executive arm of government, but would necessarily experience both an infusion of blood and some reduction in power, especially in the evaluation and formulation of policy.

In the long term, it is important not only to ensure that the senior level of the civil service does not take policy-making powers into its own hands, but also that it implements impartially policies decided by a Left-wing government. This can never happen so long as recruitment to the top civil service remains heavily class-biased.

At present the process of selection is essentially one undertaken by civil servants for civil servants, save that final selection boards have two (out of five) outside members. Recently the Select Committee on Expenditure found that all four civil service commissioners, appointed to oversee the service, were deputy or under secretaries from the Civil Service Department. Three of the four had been civil servants all their working lives. The service is in fact hopelessly inbred.

The selection procedure for the central civil service clearly needs to be far more objective and to be placed under independent supervision. The essential principle is that the public examination for entry should be conducted on an anonymous basis. The ultimate responsibility for this lies with Parliament. A cross-party parliamentary committee, with its own staff, might be a suitable body for supervising civil service regulations, administering the processes of recruitment and promotion, and approving the service's procedures for communication, accountability, planning and management.

Planning for social equality

Social equality is a major objective which would not be well served by public expenditure control, as developed since 1960 by Treasury civil servants. Public expenditure control has been the major means of preserving the *status quo*. It was developed as a by-product of economic management in order to impose upon spending departments, like those of Education and Health, a limit over a period of five years in their expansion of costs. Planning inevitably took the form of restraints on growth and incremental additions to the existing structure of services. It did not involve the fulfilment of services and benefits built on the identification of greatest need. It confirmed the supreme power of the Treasury in social policy. It also led to the absurd divorce between planning the private sector and planning the public sector.

There must be simultaneous strengthening of social planning at the centre and a big increase in participatory democracy. The need for what has been called a 'joint approach to social policy' has been increasingly acknowledged in recent years. A select committee could be established to oversee the coordination of social planning, and a social development unit, consisting of specialists recruited from outside the civil service, as well as existing civil servants, could be given a duty to work out longer-term strategies to establish social equality, marshal a range of outside expertise, and monitor and evaluate existing policies and administrative practices of both central and local departments in relation to government objectives. The select committee should consult the public at every stage and play a major part in explaining the need for certain developments.

Parliament and government

The responsibility for the activities of both ministers and civil servants lies ultimately with Parliament. We do not believe in an appointed Parliament, whether hereditary or not. All members of Parliament should be elected. Nor is a two-chamber, elected Parliament a sensible proposition because if the two chambers are in conflict each will try to veto the other. The House of Lords must therefore be abolished. Parliament should consist simply and solely of the House of Commons.

The elected House of Commons can and should make arrangements to be aided in carrying out its duties by advice and debate among other groups of people. But the need for the House of Commons to receive advice and to be aware of the views of interested parties is no justification for having a second chamber with legislative power. The need can best be served by providing the House of Commons with full facilities to make issues known, to obtain evidence, and to be aware of the expression of views and grievances from every quarter. The House of Commons should be the hub of a democratic communications system, providing the central forum for the critique of government.

The main reason why many top people want the House of Lords retained is to provide some kind of defence against a dynamic Labour government with a majority in the House of Commons. It is precisely because the House of Lords can and has been used to challenge the authority of the Commons that its abolition has become urgent. We cannot afford any compromise with the principle of representative democracy through an elected Parliament when our objectives require representative democracy to be made far more effective. The abolition of the House of Lords is a constitutional reform for which Labour must argue between now and the next general election.

Open government

The House of Commons has in fact already started to expand the powers and resources of its committees responsible for scrutinizing government activity. The single most important reform for which it now needs to press is comprehensive access to government information. The principle must be that every failure or refusal to disclose information requires to be justified. Where the justification itself involves sensitive information, the House of Commons should ask a small committee or officer of the House in whom everyone can reasonably have confidence to examine the facts of the case and reach a decision which Parliament can then enforce. MPs should continue to expand the powers of their committees to examine both government policies and legislation, but should at the same time increase their own individual powers of scrutiny by strengthening the research and secretarial facilities available to them.

A formal mechanism for requiring disclosure of information is only the beginning. A major task for a future Labour government must be to make full disclosure a normal and everyday practice in government in this country. Official secrecy, which has become a habit in public bodies, is the greatest protector of authoritarianism and obstacle to democratic accountability. What the public eye does not see, the political heart cannot grieve over. If only a few people know what the options are and the aims which policies are meant to be achieving, only a few people can comment when the policies fail or suggest that different options should be chosen. This is the insidious restriction implicit in the principle, traditionally followed, of 'need to know'. Those who 'need to know', in official practice, are those who make or carry out decisions. Others do not need to know, and had better not know, if decisions are to proceed unhindered by criticism. Yet democracy can work properly only if policy-makers tell the truth, and reveal information and decision-making processes in full. Governments will tell the whole truth only if they know that evasions and misinformation are likely to be detected. When the public call policy-makers hypocrites, they mean that they do not tell the whole truth. They are right. Policy-makers protected by secrecy continually practise hypocrisy and manipulation.

A Labour government could begin to change traditions of secrecy without legislation and without spending public money. All that is needed is openness by ministers and pressure from them for openness on the part of the top civil service. This will indeed be a test of whether ministers in a future Labour government regard democratic socialism as a practical proposition and it will determine the style and dynamic of their administration. But they must seek at the first opportunity to back up democratic practice with legislation – a Freedom of Information Act – and administrative reorganization.

At the end of the day ministers and civil servants must even be prepared to say what they don't know as well as what they do know, and to admit that, since they do not have absolute power, their policies are often compromises forced on them by other institutions.

Labour ministers, attempting the hugely difficult task of responding to the crisis into which Britain has been plunged, will have to be open if the public is to understand their failures as well as their successes.

Democracy and the media

The press and television nowadays provide the main source of information and the main forum for discussion about politics and government for most of the electorate. These media are largely a one-way affair. Most people can only read, watch and listen to what the media say without much chance of answering back. Worse still, the media are dominated by establishment views. All this constitutes an immediate obstacle to the growth and evolution of democratic socialism in Britain and presents a major, practical problem to the Labour Party. A Labour government normally has considerable opportunity to influence what is put across by the media. But even as an elected government, Labour could still easily be put in an embattled and defensive position by the media in the event of any major confrontation between the government and the establishment.

Some reforms are therefore urgent. The principle should be to encourage the independence and diversity of expression by journalists and programme makers. Open government would provide a sound base for greater independence. Press and TV journalists have learned from the United States how freedom of information laws have allowed the US press and television to explore hidden areas of executive activity. A Labour government should also abandon the unattributed lobby briefing and put its dealings with the press on an entirely open footing. Such changes would gain the goodwill of many journalists who resent their profession's complicity in the manipulation of public opinion through government's control over what information is given, and how it is given.

Constricting commercial and editorial pressures must also be weakened. Various steps could be taken to open out television and radio. One would be to reconstitute the fourth television channel as an Open Broadcasting Authority, with the specific duty of sponsoring programmes reflecting varied viewpoints, made by independent, non-commercial production groups. Another would be to reconstitute the boards of ITV companies and the BBC to make them broadly representative of the community and to convert the companies into non-profit-making trusts. A third would be to establish a charter or code for radio and television journalists and programme controllers so as to bring the rules by which programmes are selected into the open. The viewing public, quite as much as politicians and interest groups, has a major interest in knowing how daily schedules are put together and in being able to influence the procedures by which this is done.

So far as the press is concerned, similar steps need to be undertaken to make public, and justify, editorial practices and to provide journalists with more independence. Newspapers, like television companies, should be trusts, not companies, and their boards should be broadly representative of the community at large. The proceeds of advertising revenue need to be made more widely available to help the promotion of new publications. An Open Press Authority funded by a levy on advertising could undertake the task of sponsoring the launch of new papers, as well as advising on the economic problems of breaking up the monopolies which now dominate the industry.

Finally, the growth of new electronic systems, such as Prestel, Ceefax and Oracle, and other innovations may have a great impact on communications in the future. Just as with the press and broadcasting, it will be vital to ensure that they do not become propaganda instruments of prevailing commercial and institutional power. Standards of journalistic independence and open access will again be necessary.

Strengthening local democracy

The principle that people must be able to share in the decisions about how social security, social services, housing, education, health care, electricity and gas supplies, and other public services are organized and delivered at a local level is central to our vision of a democratic socialist community. Local authorities provide most of these services and take a huge number of decisions which directly affect the quality and security of people's lives. The reorganization of local government into larger and more complex units and the development of 'corporate management' techniques have together shifted the balance of power in local authorities away from elected councillors towards the senior local bureaucrats. A few committee chairmen (and they usually are men) share in this corporate control of local affairs, but most councillors, unpaid amateurs given token allowances, lack the time and resources they need to influence policies and represent their communities. A democratic balance must be created by paying councillors and giving them the research and other resources they need to carry out their duties to the public.

It is often argued that authorities should be given a strong local tax base – perhaps through a local income tax – to make them independent of central government: the point being that Whitehall provides some sixty per cent of local authority revenue, and therefore takes an often nannyish, and lately draconian, interest in how it is spent. Our view is that central government must devolve as much as it can to local democratic decision. But its responsibility for national economic planning means that it will always ultimately have the final power over the distribution of resources and revenues; be they collected nationally or locally. A socialist government is also likely, for example, to want to set minimum standards for services – later we argue the case for a massive spread of day care facilities for the under-fives – to ensure that local authorities adopt comprehensive plans for secondary education, and to stop the indiscriminate sale of council houses. In the short term at least, many deprived areas will continue to lack the resources locally which will provide a tax base broad enough to meet the needs of their local community. They will continue to depend upon a national redistribution of resources through central government grant. Indeed, generous government funding of local authorities during the 1960s and early 1970s actually allowed them great freedom to expand and experiment.

One of the major reasons why authorities are now unable to rally people to the defence of their expanded services is that they failed then to involve the community in their activities. Most of them acted as paternalistic outposts of central government. As a result, the majority of people do not even know exactly what services their local councils provide, let alone share in the decisions about how they should be provided. A future Labour government should extend the freedom and powers of local authorities – especially in local industrial and economic planning – and should possibly hand over functions which other public bodies provide. But it has to be on terms which would involve the local community. Our freedom of information law would extend to local authorities (and to other public undertakings, such as nationalized industries, electricity and gas boards, social security offices). Local authorities should be legally obliged to give access to housing, social services, school and other files to the individual people affected by them, and should institute agreed data protection procedures to protect their confidentiality. Finally, while the local government Ombudsman's powers to investigate and control maladministration should be strengthened, and people should be given direct access to the Ombudsman, there is a huge need to integrate and strengthen existing complaints procedures to give people who feel aggrieved or harmed by a local authority's decision a real opportunity to have their case examined.

Labour authorities could make a start with such proposals now (as, indeed, some have done). We would like to see local communities invited now to share in strategic decision-making over housing, social services and other plans, and then to be engaged (at a neighbourhood level) in the delivery and management of services and more local decisions. Neighbourhood councils with real powers, and the accountability which should accompany them, could be set up. Later, in Chapter 14, we put forward more detailed proposals for the involvement of local people in social services. Our general principle is that all public services – including the police, social security, gas and electricity boards, and water undertakings – should be decentralized and democratized. There is every reason, for example, why local social security and employment offices should be made accountable locally. Ideas and experiments must be allowed to grow up from grassroots level to influence local, regional and national decision-making. A socialist approach would leave room for plans to evolve through an interaction of theory, decision and experience, through experiments, local struggles and popular demands.

The rule of law

The legal system should not only be the means whereby Parliament's writ is enforced but also the basic protector of individual liberties, including the right to dissent. Unfortunately it tends to have another role, justified in the name of public order but in practice exercised mainly to limit dissent and to keep people in line with 'higher authority'. The security services, the police and the courts are only very weakly subject to democratic control. They are, as we showed in Chapter 7, biased in class terms; they often become instruments of oppression.

When the forces of law and order are repressive and not themselves subject to effective democratic control, democracy itself can all too easily be put in jeopardy. The fear of repression can frighten people and discourage them from the expression of views which is essential if democracy is to be effective. Protests may never be heard and injustices may easily pass unperceived by those who are not themselves affected.

Security services

Constitutionally the security and intelligence services (MI5 and MI6) are accountable to the Prime Minister, the Home Secretary or the Foreign Minister. Since these ministers habitually refuse to be answerable to Parliament in respect of the security services, democratic accountability begins and ends there. Too little is known about the security services to assess exactly how far they endanger liberty, or to propose precise reforms. A thorough study should be made by a select committee to identify the problems more accurately.

First, the services must be accountable to Parliament as well as to individual ministers. For example, an annual report could be published on the general functions, resources and activities of the services and the directors could be examined on their reports by a parliamentary committee. Second, there must be clear limits and safeguards laid down by law on the clandestine methods used by the security and intelligence services. It would be desirable also that their files should be subject to some system of verification and weeding as is now done in some other countries (when such procedures were applied to the Special Branch in New South Wales, ninety per cent of the files were shredded). If these services are put on a legal basis, their functions should be confined to matters of genuine national security. They must be prohibited from policing private opinions or political and trade union activities. This would involve a total transformation of their roles.

The police

The police also lack sufficient democratic accountability. It is generally agreed that police must be independent in enforcing the criminal law in particular cases. But as long ago as 1962 a royal commission expressed concern about other activities 'over which neither a police authority nor anyone else at present appears to have recognized powers of control over a chief constable and in respect of which the chief constable is not ordinarily brought to account'. These activities included his general decisions on the policing of an area, the disposition of the force, the concentration of resources, the handling of political demonstrations and of industrial disputes, and so on. It is anomalous that, because the Home Secretary is the police authority for the Metropolitan area, these matters are his responsibility for which he is to some extent accountable to Parliament. Outside London the chief constable is not accountable to his police authority for these matters, except in the most general way through annual reports and any other reports the authority may be successful in obtaining from him.

The obvious democratic answer is to make the chief constable answerable to the local police authority in all matters except individual prosecutions, exactly like any other local government officer. The authority should be composed entirely of directly elected members. This system should be extended to London, where there is no local accountability, and Northern Ireland. The chief constable's accountability should include decisions about the general disposition of the police force, policies about prosecutions against classes of people or activities, as well as the appointment, promotion and discipline of individual officers. The chief constable could be entitled to withhold information from the authority only with the Home Secretary's approval.

The Royal Commission on Criminal Procedure has recommended that new Crown Prosecutors should take over the duty of prosecutions from the police. We support this proposal. Even if this happens, policy on prosecutions will still have to be determined in an accountable way and the relationship between the police and prosecutors will have to be carefully supervised.

The procedure for dealing with specific complaints about police conduct, where the chief officer is answerable to the Police Complaints Board, is still widely distrusted. The local Ombudsman service is best placed to carry out this task in a truly independent way (although it would need new powers and staff to do so).

If the police are made accountable to elected authorities and complaints are dealt with in a genuinely independent way, they will have a much clearer mandate for activities which, inevitably, sometimes make them unpopular with particular groups of people. At the same time there will be less possibility of oppressive action by the police if elected councillors could and would lose votes as a consequence.

The courts

The final issue we must consider here is adjudication by the courts. At present the judiciary is a hierarchical and unaccountable institution. Judges are appointed almost entirely from members of the bar. They are selected in secrecy, and totally subjectively, in accordance with the Lord Chancellor's impression of the views of existing judges about barristers whom they happen to know. In effect, judges are a self-selecting clique. Another problem is that the imposing system of the courts is so expensive that it has become almost inaccessible to private citizens, except when they are forced to appear as defendants.

The most urgent reform is to broaden out the process of selection and break down barriers within the legal profession. Judges should be selected by a commission, appointed by Parliament, which includes not only representatives of the legal profession but also laymen from relevant interest groups. The monopoly of barristers in the higher courts and senior legal appointments should be broken by fusing the whole legal profession (barristers and solicitors) into one, and ending the antiquated system of patronage which governs entry to the bar. As well as reducing the exclusivity of the bar and judiciary, this reform would reduce costs for customers and arguably improve legal services. At local level, too, the covert system for the appointment of magistrates should be replaced by a more open and representative procedure, akin to that which we have recommended for the appointment of judges.

The basic trouble with the courts is that they have become inward-looking and oppressive relics of the past (though some county courts deserve to be excepted from this general stricture). They are run as hierarchical institutions, remote from the community, in which anyone other than a member of the legal profession feels an outsider. A degree of procedural formality is a good idea: people must know what to expect and how to conduct themselves. But the courts should become less forbidding and less technical: they should regard themselves as providing a service to the community and, in time, they should become part of that community, and accountable to it. One immediate change might take the lead: we badly need a family court within which all matters to do with family law – divorce, separation, maintenance, marital property, access to and care of children, and so on – are brought together and determined in an atmosphere which is not so inimical to friendly settlement as the existing structure.

Equality before the law

But reform would have to dig deeper if we are to make a reality of the notion of equality before the law. The means-tested legal aid scheme fails to ensure this principle: it assists only the poorest, and does not extend to tribunals, which have a caseload six times heavier than that of the civil courts on issues of fundamental importance to working-class people, like employment, housing, social security, immigration. Few solicitors do much civil legal aid work, and those who do concentrate on matrimonial cases; fewer still practise in working-class areas. Most solicitors rely on conveyancing and commercial work. Meanwhile, the work of citizens' advice bureaux and the handful of surviving law centres indicates that there is a huge unmet need for legal assistance in housing, employment, welfare rights and immigration cases. We need an independent legal services commission, with a lay majority, to finance law centres and general advice services, like CABs, with solicitors, and to employ solicitors in areas of greatest need or as an alternative to private practices. Law centres provide the best way forward: they are accountable locally, take on educational and group work (for tenants' associations, for example), advertise their services and specialize in the particular problems of their area. They also combine the talents of legal and non-legal workers. The solicitors' monopoly in conveyancing should be ended. As conveyancing supplies over half the profits of the average firm, this should encourage private solicitors to take on caseloads more representative of local needs, and might make salaried service – and legal aid work – more attractive for more solicitors. Solicitors should also be allowed to advertise. The commission would also take over the running of the legal aid scheme from the Law Society and consider how the funds might be most efficiently spent: the principle should be to get legal aid to people who most need it, and not to inflate legal fees. The legal aid budget would necessarily rise, but if people's understanding of the law and their ability to make use of legal services and the courts is strengthened, then in time there should be less need for recourse to both.

In the cause of equality before the law, we must finally put to an end the shameful racist character of our citizenship and immigration law. The government's Nationality Act has been designed ultimately to remove the openly racist notion of 'patriality' (which means descent from a white-born British ancestor) from our immigration law, but to maintain strict immigration control against black people through a morass of detailed regulations defining citizenship. All countries maintain control of immigration, and it is entirely legitimate for Britain to continue to do so. But a future Labour government must act at once to make our immigration (and citizenship) law non-racist. The key to this is quite simple: the government must abolish the new 'British overseas' category of citizenship which the act has created. This is a second-class status, specially designed to keep black British citizens abroad, mostly Asians in East Africa, out of Britain. Second, the government must restore to those few thousand Asians in East Africa with British citizenship the right of settlement here. With the removal of a few extra petty regulations, Britain would then have a non-racist immigration law.

The way that law is operated would also require changes. Inevitably, anyone who wants entry to Britain must show that they have the right to settle here. But they, in turn, must have a right to a sympathetic and objective hearing of their case if their eligibility is in doubt. Instead, the immigration rules are applied and interpreted in the most restrictive manner possible, and an unreasonably exacting burden of proof is demanded. People who are already resident here, and who are accused of being illegal immigrants, are again assumed to be 'guilty' unless they can prove their 'innocence'. This contradicts the tradition, inherent in our law, that an accused person is innocent until proved guilty: the burden of proof must be reversed. Most appeals by people refused entry are heard by adjudicators, appointed by the Home Secretary (who is party to the case), in the absence of the appellant. And nasty and prejudicial decisions and breaches of natural justice have been justified by a judiciary which is blinded by its own cant. The processes of immigration must be made simpler and faster, and not exploited as an obstacle, and the administration of immigration law must be liberalized. Both should be removed from the charge of the Home Office bureaucracy, which is by now too compromised to be trusted to run them in an impartial and just spirit, and handed over to an immigration and naturalization board, one of whose duties would be to offer an advisory and counselling service. The board should be directly accountable to Parliament.

Towards a powerful society
The reforms set out here are modest and will not, of themselves, bring about democratic government in Britain. They are only a first step in that direction. As we demonstrated in earlier chapters, political power in Britain is concentrated in a small group, most of the members of which are not elected. They survive changes of government. Their work, on the record of the past, is not even much affected by changes of government. They will not easily be made accountable. Nor must we forget that even elected members of public bodies may not always be concerned to promote the public interest. The principles of election and accountability are not sufficient, although they are necessary, safeguards. The only sure safeguard rests finally in a self-confident and united community which is prepared to defend its democratic rights. Our immediate strategy is to use the centralized power of a democratized state, in alliance with a majority of the population and organized labour movement, to create a fairer and more equal society. Our ultimate aim must be to achieve a powerful society with a minimal state – a socialist society. We will not achieve that society merely by improving the machinery of democracy. But if that machinery is badly defective there is no way in which socialism can be achieved. The first step is to force our rulers to account for their actions. It is a measure of how

far we have to go that, today, they are still able to exercise their power largely unembarrassed by representations of the kind made in this chapter.

12 Common ownership and industrial democracy

It was no accident that clause four of the Labour Party's constitution defined the socialist goal of common ownership in democratic terms:

To secure for the workers by hand or by brain the full fruits of their industry and the most equitable distribution thereof that may be possible upon the basis of common ownership of the means of production, distribution and exchange, and the best obtainable system of popular administration and control of each industry and service.

Those early members of the Labour Party chose to say 'common ownership' – not nationalization or state control. The phrase 'the best obtainable system of popular administration and control of each industry or service' is the very opposite of the bureaucratic centralist control of the economy which characterizes the regimes of Eastern Europe and the Soviet Union, as well as of the centralized bureaucratic corporations, private and public, which dominate our own economy with only the barest pretence of accountability.

In the last chapter, we set out proposals to make a reality of representative government. But political democracy alone is not enough. Workers of all kinds – in offices as on the shop floor – need a new franchise at work. People who give their work and lives to industry, commerce, public utilities and public services should not be excluded from the right to shape and plan the work they do, to share in the decisions about the future of the enterprises to which they contribute and to secure for themselves, their children and their communities a greater security. In this chapter, we reassert the Labour Party's original goal of common ownership, but we recognize that common ownership alone would not achieve the extension of democratic rights we seek. The transfer of power must not be to government alone; that power must be shared with the workers in the commonly owned enterprises and with the community at large. Here, therefore, we try to provide a perspective for the gradual transformation of the institutions of the mixed economy – both publicly and privately owned – into a system of common ownership and democratic planning of the economy. The institutional pattern of a democratic socialist economy will have to emerge from experience. It cannot be decided on the basis of abstract discussion. In this chapter, we seek to identify some guidelines, based on what has happened in the past, and to clarify some issues which are now particularly crucial. It is noticeable that public debate on these issues is often highly ideological, contrary to the pragmatic approach which is supposed to be characteristic of British thinking. We must be concerned here with practical questions. We begin with the contribution that the trade union tradition of collective bargaining, and Labour's developing industrial strategy, might make.

The democratic advance towards a democratic socialist society is a long struggle. What is best at one stage may not be good enough later. Thus common ownership and popular administration and control are objectives which must be fulfilled by degrees. Progress towards these objectives has to start now within the framework of our present mixed economy. The circumstances vary enormously – from those of small firms to giant multinationals and nationalized industries, from services to heavy manufacturing. The strongest historical foundations for advance are those of collective bargaining on the one side and government management of the economy on the other. But these are not the only traditions from which we can start, and there are difficult questions to be faced along the way.

The labour movement's democratic perspective

All ideas are shaped and coloured by experience. In countries where the working class has not developed as a decisive force, and where in consequence the people have not won and consolidated democratic rights, socialist thinking may well look to a strategy of seizing power rather than winning, and using, power by democratic means. We argued in Chapter 9 against insurrectionary tactics in principle. They are also wholly alien to the traditions of British socialism. Labour socialism in Britain emerged from a working class that pioneered trade unionism, and has steadily increased its political strength ever since the class structure of our society polarized under the impact of industrialization. The labour movement saw representative democracy as the means by which the interests of working people could be advanced, and played an important part in establishing basic democratic rights in Britain. The movement won a degree of power, and still more potential power, which earned or compelled respect. The rights of assembly, free speech, free worship and free publication are all part of the movement's battle colours. So also is the right of collective bargaining. The concepts of freedom and democracy for which the movement pressed were not viewed abstractly. They included rights in work, education, health and housing. Civil rights and freedom from poverty were seen as two sides of the same coin.

The main way in which workers have extended their influence in industry has been through collective bargaining with employers, organized through a trade union framework. It is often tacitly assumed, as for example in the discussions of the Bullock committee of inquiry during the period of the last Labour Government, that collective bargaining reaches some kind of limit beyond which the further development of industrial democracy must be based on some quite different approach, such as the appointment of worker directors. But there is no evidence to support such an assumption. Indeed, there is ample evidence that collective bargaining still has a vast unrealized potential. The shop stewards at the Upper Clyde Shipbuilders in the early 1970s ended up negotiating with the government on the whole future of the business where they worked. The miners recently forced Mrs Thatcher to reverse policies which threatened the coal industry. Many other similar cases could be cited. Nowadays nearly every wage battle develops into a public debate on the causes of cost inflation, the role of market forces and the strategy of the industry concerned. The point is that the narrow wage-orientated role of trade unions has been broadened out by the deepening crisis of our economy. Reality forces trade unionists to extend their critique and assert their right to a say on matters that go far beyond those areas previously regarded as the proper scope for negotiation. Collective bargaining is the main vehicle by which industrial democracy is now developing. It has generated a new and powerful leadership at shop floor level. However well-meaning, mechanisms developed from outside, like putting a few workers on the board, might weaken trade unionism by placing workers' representatives in an ambivalent position with respect to management or to the state.

The development of industrial democracy

That is not to say that a Labour government cannot help the development of industrial democracy. Legislation should aim to expand the role of collective bargaining and establish the rights of organized workers to a greater say in the running of their industry. Compulsory planning agreements, in which the trade unions, management and government are equally involved in determining companies' future plans, would give workers a strong bargaining lever. But they must avoid the pitfall described by a trade unionist who was involved in the last Labour Government's single planning agreement with a private company: 'The basic problem . . . is that you are in a planning area, talking about minor amendments to what is essentially management's corporate plan. You're not autonomous.' Disclosure of information must also extend beyond government to private business and industry. Companies must be obliged by law to disclose comprehensive information to trade unions on a regular basis and in advance of any major decision. There should be no area of decision-making in a company or industry which is closed to collective bargaining. The objective must be to include investment strategy, the allocation of capital spending, manpower planning and much more.

Collective bargaining would then offer much more positive advantages. Only a few workers have in the past participated in industrial-democratic experiments. A strategy of union bargaining could involve the rank and file in discussion and action, to allow them to experience themselves as intelligent and skilled people, and to construct and bargain for alternative plans.

Government legislation of this kind would of course meet determined resistance from industry. In 1975, the CBI announced that it regarded 'as non-negotiable any attempt to subject the leading 100 companies to a planning agreement system'. Leading industrialists were equally opposed to the government's proposals for disclosure of information of a far less radical nature than we envisage. The CBI told Labour MPs that companies would refuse to give unions the information, even if they were obliged to do so by law. Even the recommendations of Bullock, which would have led to the incorporation of worker-directors into managerial perspectives, were unacceptable to industry. We recognize, therefore, that the changes we advocate cannot be brought about by parliamentary action alone. The labour movement must begin to build now on the existing strength of the shop steward movement to build up understanding and support at shop floor and office level for Labour's democratic industrial strategy so that it can be sustained when a Labour government is in power. Nor should we assume that management would be uniformly opposed to such proposals.

The argument is sometimes advanced that only the 'strong' – that is, the well-organized – can reap benefits from collective bargaining. This argument is usually advanced to win backing for policies of wage restraint, but it gains well-meaning adherence among people who would broadly sympathize with the aims we set out in this book. Implicitly, it is assumed that the 'weak' would do better if collective bargaining were restrained or even if trade unionism were dismantled. This is a dangerous nonsense. Whenever and wherever collective bargaining has been suppressed or placed in abeyance, the interests of all workers have grievously suffered. There are poorly organized sectors and groups, and we put forward proposals to raise their earnings and working conditions in the next chapter. But essentially their need is for help with their difficulties, including lack of funds and weak organization, so that they can develop their own leadership. To suggest that high-paid workers are responsible for the plight of the low-paid is nonsense. A low-paid worker points inescapably to a low-paying employer. The trade union movement's responsibility is to strengthen the organization of weaker groups and to support their efforts to obtain higher wages and better working conditions.

Organizing for change

The interdependence of industries in modern society gives organized workers strong leverage, but power in collective bargaining derives mainly from having a good case and enjoying the support of others. For example, in the 1950s and 1960s the miners were persuaded that coal was in decline and as an industrial force they were dormant for nearly twenty years. But when in 1972 and 1973–4 they engaged in a major confrontation with the government, they were able to win through on the basis of the massive solidarity of other organized workers, demonstrated in supportive actions which the Conservatives have ever since sought to outlaw. The strike of the Post Office workers in 1971 is a good example of the defeat which a major trade union can suffer if others stand by without giving significant support.

The potential of collective bargaining can only be realized if trade unions are strong. Insularity and competitiveness stand in the way of stronger trade unionism when power is crystallized in rival structures, each of which jealously guards its autonomy. Leaders can then become obsessed with the interests and influence of their own union and negotiate amalgamations as a means of empire-building. The criteria for trade union amalgamating structures can often be the status and career interests of their bureaucracies. The General Council of the TUC can at times be like a gathering of suspicious tribal chiefs.

We recognize that the trade unions are far more democratically organized than any other comparable large-scale institutions in the country, be they private companies, nationalized industries, insurance companies, building societies or pressure groups like the Automobile Association, the Civic Trust and even Shelter. Accountability is built into the structure of trade unions and the TUC. Nevertheless, undemocratic practices – like the appointment of union presidents for life – have been incorporated into trade union constitutions, democratic structures have been allowed to ossify, and some trade union officials have lost sight of the basic principles of accountability. The issue of how trade union power should best be consolidated in new democratic structures is crucial and too little discussed. The labour movement is often afraid to offend leaders whose influence on votes cast at the TUC congress or Labour Party conference is so great. But such silence is a dangerous form of political opportunism. Undemocratic unions, however large or powerful, cannot be vehicles for an expansion of democracy. The campaign for democratic accountability in the Labour Party can only fully succeed if accompanied by a similar process within trade unions. The paradox of union leaders, subject to periodic re-election, voting against the same principle for MPs as representatives of the Labour Party is only equalled by that of union leaders, elected or appointed for life, who are advocates of mandatory re-selection of MPs.

Apart from the general issue of advancing democracy within trade unions, there are specific problems of industrial structure. In many industries there is coordinated negotiation at national level and at plant level, but no combined institution for negotiation at the company level, which is where the most crucial decisions are taken. The TUC quite rightly wants unions to have access to company information. It would seem impossible to use such information effectively without coordinated institutions for company bargaining. Planning agreements as envisaged by the Labour Party would be on a company basis. Extension of the scope of collective bargaining depends on development of company negotiations.

The trade unions will need to give an explicit constitutional status to the 'combine committees' – the combined inter-union shop stewards' committees – for bargaining at company level. Otherwise, negotiations conducted between union officers and company executives will be handed down to workers and shop stewards on a take-it-or-leave-it basis. Some trade union leaders oppose combine committees as tending to undermine their own authority. But if the leaders' authority is at variance with the views and opinions of shop stewards, it might be that the leadership is at variance with the workers from whom its authority is supposed to derive. The best known of the combine committees is probably the Lucas Aerospace combine which was formed (as they themselves put it) in response to the lessons in the three Rs – 'reorganization, rationalization, redundancy' – which Lucas workers learned in the early 1970s. The combine covered all thirteen unions at the company's seventeen sites and finally produced their own alternative plan for socially useful production. Among their proposals was a prototype 'hobcart' designed to give mobility to children suffering from spina bifida. There are now, however, some two dozen multi-union combines, organized at company or industry level, most of which have prepared their own plans for their companies or industries. In short, a new type of trade union activity is growing up which is creating a sense of power and self-confidence among workers. This rank-and-file activity should be encouraged and developed, and involved in drawing up Labour's industrial plans, now and when Labour is in government.

The role of common ownership

There are two fundamental objections to the mixed economy, as it exists in Britain today. One is that the power it accords to the City, top management and senior civil servants perpetuates the class system and is the primary source of inequality in our society. The other is that the mixed economy no longer works: it does not deliver jobs, wages, pensions, public services or even profits. The Social Democrats who have broken away from the Labour Party have publicly made a commitment to the mixed economy into a supposed sticking point of principle. The fact is that this commitment is simply to the *status quo*. The party's industrial strategy – of which common ownership is a central component – does not envisage the demise of the mixed economy, but seeks to make the mixture richer with the injection of more publicly owned and democratically run enterprise. We recognize that consumer choice is a significant instrument of democracy. Hundreds of thousands of private businesses would survive, though we would prefer to see most of those with more than one or two employees transformed into cooperatives (and our proposals on wealth in Chapter 13 are designed to bring that about).

Under Labour's existing strategy, common ownership and public investment would be selectively extended in manufacturing industry. The idea is that these commonly owned companies would, through increased investment, act as leaders in the various sectors of industry. The National Enterprise Board would also intervene to create new industries or enterprises, to guide the development of new technology and to influence the regional distribution of industry through common ownership and public investment. Secondly, planning agreements would be negotiated, as we have seen, between the top 100 companies, the government and relevant trade unions. These compulsory agreements would cover strategic decisions on investment, employment, location of production, price policy and the like, and the government would be able to call in aid as bargaining counters a variety of financial sanctions and inducements. The government would also take powers to plan the economy and control the financial institutions to ensure that the resources needed for a substantial increase in industrial investment would be at hand.

The case for common ownership here rests largely on efficiency. Our concern in this chapter is with accountability. Common ownership can substitute collective interests, represented in Parliament, for the narrow class interests of the top people who control the major financial institutions and large companies. Commonly owned enterprises and services, in principle, exist to serve the whole population: they can be made accountable both to the public, through Parliament and decentralized management with consumer representation built in, and to their workforces, through worker representation at all levels and continuing collective bargaining. By contrast, profitability is the overriding principle of large-scale private organizations; and they are effectively run by self-appointing cliques accountable, if at all, to headquarters overseas or to financial interests in the City.

By these standards, postwar nationalization has made a disappointing contribution to the reconstruction of our society. Its managements have become highly centralized. The power of the top managers within the industries, and of the top civil servants with whom they negotiate, has been reinforced. In the mixed economy, they have been largely forced to adopt the criteria of the market – under Labour as under Conservative governments. In a real sense, they are still, after nationalization, a power base for the same ruling establishment. They are also popularly regarded as being bureaucratic – with some justice – and inefficient – which is, overall, far from fair. We cannot conclude from this experience that it is better to leave major enterprises in the hands of the City and multinational companies. Rather we must face up to the task of making common ownership publicly accountable. One way would be for existing state enterprises to take a lead in the development of workers' control. Public service unions could demand, through collective bargaining, involvement at all levels in nationalized industries and public utilities, up to and including the boards. They should also seek representation of wider community interests and closer accountability to Parliament. They could demand now full disclosure of information prior to critical decisions being taken, and a full share in strategic planning. An incoming Labour government could appoint new managers, charged to make the industries more accountable and to decentralize decision-making. The top jobs should be advertised and workers should sit on the interviewing panels. The recommended appointees could be scrutinized by the appropriate select committee of the Commons which should have the power to veto the appointment. Going beyond this, further common ownership could be designed from the outset as an intermediate stage in the process of converting national or multinational enterprises into organizations which were accountable both to the public and their workers.

Cooperatives are another type of social ownership which needs strong backing from the Labour Party in national and local government and from the trade unions. During the 1970s, when work-ins and factory occupations were a frequent response to plant closures, workers' cooperatives were a much-discussed solution. In several cases, of which Triumph Meriden remains the best known example, workers' cooperatives were set up. But the civil service was hostile to them and, though the public funds advanced to them were well publicized, they were usually underfinanced and received less than more conventional private enterprises would have done. But the experience of workers taking control of their own factories has advanced our confidence in what can be achieved, and many Labour councils are already committed to advancing cooperative enterprises at local level.

Ultimately, it is natural in principle to look to workers' control as the primary route for accountability of management in a society within which common ownership was widespread. The most direct interests at stake in managerial decisions are usually those of employees. Ideally, we could imagine an economy where all the large businesses were owned and controlled by the workers, with the government's responsibility confined to planning the economy as a whole. General planning instruments would be operated in accordance with principles determined by Parliament. The enterprises' strategies, taxes and subsidies would be negotiated between the government and worker-controlled enterprises under published planning agreements which could be freely criticized and brought up for amendment in Parliament when necessary. A co-ordinated, but decentralized, scheme of this kind seems to offer a better prospect of accountability than the *status quo* in government today where top management and the civil service wield largely invisible and unaccountable power or a large network of state-owned industries.

The use of democratic power

Shop stewards and trade unions have often tried to set out their vision of how their industries should be developed. The plans formulated by Lucas and Vickers workers in the 1970s are well-known examples of such perspectives. The themes of such thinking are summed up in the phrase 'socially useful production', which contrasts with production for profit in an unplanned market system. Few people, if they have the choice, really want to make arms for export to feed wars and repression in other parts of the world. Nor do they want their production to be determined solely by essentially trivial dictates of artificially contrived consumerism. Nor, finally, do most people enjoy producing by inefficient methods or in situations of excess capacity or overmanning.

But we cannot conclude from these observations that the growth of workers' power, plant by plant, company by company, will automatically make our economy efficient and its products more socially useful. Workers will still face the market pressures and financial constraints which now impinge on management, although they could make different choices within those constraints. Nor could

177

a socialist government simply provide unlimited credit to render financial constraints inoperative. Between the harsh dictates of a theoretical 'pure' market system and the anarchy of production without any regard for cost or profit there lie many possibilities for planning industry and the economy with more or less independence from market forces and varying degrees of decentralization.

Some examples indicate the range of choice. At one extreme, the health service in government is funded almost entirely by the state and operated on non-market criteria. In other spheres, such as defence procurement, telecommunications, railways and other public utilities, we have highly regulated public sector markets. A wide range of social choice could be exercised about how services were provided, although in recent years they have increasingly been operated according to the accounting criteria of the City and private industry. Then there are the managed markets of large multinational companies which have considerable control over prices and are able to plan innovation and investment on a long-term basis, with little accountability to any outside body so long as they continue to make profits. Such companies are frequently in conflict with trade unions and governments precisely because their managements do actually have wide discretion in their response to market developments. Small businesses are on the whole far more strictly constrained in their decisions by immediate market opportunities and financial pressures. In this situation, collective bargaining has less direct leverage unless it is backed up by government action to change the economic conditions of the industry. Most sectors are in fact influenced by various types of government intervention, including subsidies, taxes and regulations. Some of these, notably financial aid and planning consents, are negotiated case by case.

The existing mixed economy is, therefore, complex and does not conform readily to any stereotype. Typically, it is a managed market system. As we have pointed out, within that system the effective power of the government to plan the economy as a whole has waned in the past

178

twenty years while the influence of multinational business and global markets has dramatically increased. Our immediate objectives for this mixed economy must be to provide greater freedom for collective bargaining to influence the development of industries by reducing market constraints and at the same time to increase the power of democratic government to plan and coordinate the whole.

The role of government

The government has two different kinds of task to perform in the building of a socialist economic system. The first is to help bring into being democratic management and common ownership of private industrial, commercial and other organizations, and then to give the new institutions continuing support. The other is to take specific responsibility for managing key aspects of the country's economic performance. We have already discussed how a Labour government might achieve the first objectives; but the government could also help enlarge the scope and freedom of democratic management through economic planning by assisting the organization of markets, by providing funds and by relaxing strict accountancy criteria. A Labour government, representing the working class, the unemployed and underprivileged, would also have to operate a planning system which allowed social equality to take priority and reduced the markets to instruments rather than arbiters of our society.

The government's immediate role in economic planning to rescue this country from our deep-seated economic crisis was discussed in Chapter 10. There we argued for a specific pattern of controls over finance, trade and industry, primarily designed to bring about a rapid recovery of business activity, to restore full employment and to rebuild the welfare state. Our priorities were investment and modernization to create reindustrialization of the economy as a whole; and the preservation and expansion of employment in the worst-hit areas. In the longer run, the aims and techniques of government planning will inevitably need to alter in response to changes in the nature of key problems in our evolving economy. It might conceivably happen, from time to time when the economy is prospering, that planning need not play any major role. But in general we must expect that there will be substantial problems of one kind and another which will require active government intervention if they are to be resolved. To this extent, management of the economy will have to remain centralized, and be made democratically accountable through national politics and Parliament. But we have to avoid the growth of unnecessary bureaucratic power at the centre. The planning objectives of government must be specifically defined and continuously scrutinized. We must ensure that they are focused on functions and issues which really matter and cannot be readily devolved. The main guarantee of this – which was discussed in Chapter 11 – would be genuinely open government, allowing the choices and issues involved to be widely publicized and debated on the basis of realistic information.

Many people worry that a planned economy might create a more authoritarian and bureaucratic society, or that it would adversely affect our relations with other countries. But planning which takes the form of open bargaining between government, management and trade unions under a changed set of rules, and perhaps ultimately between government and worker-controlled enterprises – always with the safeguards of elections, collective bargaining and consumer representation – should open out the opportunities for public debate and meaningful action without restricting the freedom of citizens as individuals. By expanding the range of possible choices, it should increase our collective freedom. Indeed, 'invisible' hands of unregulated market mechanisms, and their more visible institutional policemen, at present severely limit freedom of personal and collective choice for all but the few who are wealthy enough to ignore the dictates of money.

Much the same considerations apply to Britain's relations with other countries. Nowadays these are mainly governed by market forces and multinational business and

180

banking. As a country, we trade with and lend to or borrow from most other countries on exclusively commercial criteria, regardless of morality or justice. Our companies sell arms for oil, oil for cars, cars for copper or uranium, without thought of the political and social consequences. With government controls over foreign exchange and imports, and with effective bargaining powers *vis-à-vis* multinationals, new choices would open up. We could make political decisions about our relationships with Europe, the United States, Japan and the Third World.

Employment for all

Finally, the economic and social objectives must be fully integrated. The recovery of the economy, along the lines we have indicated, will lead to a large reduction in unemployment, greater job security and higher wages. But a positive employment policy will have to be developed in other respects to create a more open access to employment. We should advance from the concept of 'full employment' to one which might more appropriately be described as 'employment for all'. People who want work, including women, older people and disabled people, should be guaranteed rights to employment.

A Labour government will need to promote new forms of industry on a large scale. But it will also have to foster the expansion of employment in the public services, and especially services like home nursing and caring day centres. The job creation, youth opportunities and other programmes which have been developed since the mid-1970s have been peripheral and largely self-defeating gestures rather than anything which could be called an employment programme. In place of a strategy designed to give least offence to the private sector, we must evolve a strategy to define the kind of employment which ought to exist in a socialist society. There must be widespread and vigorous debate about how we can create more jobs of the kind which everyone recognizes to be socially useful, productive and satisfactory to the people who undertake them.

13 From him that hath

In the first part of this book we showed how our society and politics have been founded on inequalities of wealth, income and power which give top people huge influence and which secure the loyalty of managerial and professional classes to existing institutions.

If we are to move towards a truly democratic society, everyone must have opportunities to participate effectively in the goods, services and responsibilities which society can provide, but from which many are at present excluded. There are various ways in which opportunities to participate can be expanded. We have already discussed how wider and more effective democracy could be achieved in the management of government, business and public services. In the next chapter, we shall examine how a Labour government could create more equal access to the more traditional social benefits and services. For the future, the labour movement must also consider how other services, like public transport, amenities and types of consumption which contribute to people's well-being, might be extended. The principle of free and cheap travel for the elderly and children has already partially been established. But now and in the future, the possession of personal income is bound to remain the most important single determinant of people's individual opportunities.

In this chapter we consider how the very great inequalities of income and wealth which endure in our present society ought to be tackled. We argue the case for structural change in the distribution of incomes and for the effective socialization of wealth. One of our principal themes is the need to raise low wages and benefits to a new minimum level of income, the 'participation' standard, which all would receive, and simultaneously to limit high incomes. More immediately, we need to simplify and strengthen taxation of incomes above the minimum level.

The need for structural charge

The ethic which inspires our view of income distribution must be contrasted with that implicit in present society. It is normal today to think of income as belonging in the first instance to the individual who earns or receives it. The payment of tax to redistribute income to others is seen as an act of collective charity, designed to mitigate poverty and help out the 'less fortunate'. This approach is based on the assumption that, in a market economy, those who receive most have contributed most to the community's well-being – and that, by implication, those who get least contribute least. Inequality is thus legitimized.

The proposals which follow start from a different conception. We see income and wealth as being generated collectively. It is only through the cooperative efforts of countless people in the past and present that any of us are able to earn the income and enjoy the wealth, private and public, that we have today. We see no particular moral value in the money earnings which people happen to receive through their jobs or through 'market' activities. We do not regard rents, profits or even pay as the natural prerogative of those who receive them. All incomes are part of a social product which passes through the hands of individuals.

Redistribution of income to provide opportunities for all is a natural and proper counterpart of the state of mutual interdependence in which we live.

Postwar social democrats have wrongly assumed that redistribution could be brought about without major changes in the basic structure of pre-tax earnings and wealth. Our argument is that it is not good enough simply to seek to modify distribution through taxation and state benefits: wealth and pre-tax earnings must be more equitably distributed in the first place. The original distribution of both has effects, socially and psychologically, which obstruct attempts to modify or redistribute income through the tax system. There are now immense inequalities of wealth and earnings. Worse still, it is assumed that benefits paid to those not in employment should be lower than the earnings of those in work. Pensions and sickness benefits as well as unemployment benefit have generally been pitched at subsistence levels only. The low paid, who are poor when they are in work, find their poverty persisting in sickness, unemployment, disability and old age. The moderate redistribution provided by the welfare state, financed by taxation of ordinary workers and not just the rich, has failed to banish mass poverty. A major reduction in inequalities of wealth and earnings is needed, not only to help the low paid, but also to be compatible with an adequate basic income for people not in work.

The income and wealth of the rich must be lowered at the same time as the income of the poor is increased. The question we now consider is how this might best be done.

A 'participation' standard

A realistic minimum standard of income must be adopted both for wage-earners and for the majority of our population who do not work. The minimum we seek might be called a 'participation' standard to distinguish it from the subsistence standard adopted after the war. The subsistence standard, which still lies at the heart of payments meted out to the poor, fails to recognize that needs are social, and not merely physical. We want a new right for all to share fully in the life of the community. This requires a recognition of the many roles people play as citizens, workers, parents, householders, neighbours and members of a local community. For example not only must parents keep their children at school at least until they are sixteen, providing money for their support, but they are expected to conform with social expectations in affording uniforms, sports kits, instruments for lessons, and various facilities at home. Parents on low incomes often cut down on food rather than fail to meet such obligations. Old people are grandparents and great-grandparents. They are also citizens who have the right as well as the need to keep up with new information. The participation standard therefore has to be worked out in terms of contemporary society rather than the society of yesterday. Those who need support in Britain today are not living in the 1950s or the 1930s and their incomes should not be decided according to some historical benchmark from the past.

The purchasing power of the poor in the United States is quite high by comparison with the average net incomes of manual workers in Britain. Yet they are very deprived in relation to the standards, expectations and obligations defined or customary in American society. The fact that there is substantial genuine poverty in this sense in the United States provides a warning to those in Britain who argue that our society can be made more equal through economic growth alone. For growth can create new forms of deprivation. And it can put today's poor at a disadvantage by allowing the rich and the prosperous to secure amenities, standards and styles of life which are out of reach of those with low incomes.

It is now widely recognized that chemical plants and motorways can create deprivation and risks to the health of people who live alongside them. The almost imperceptible development of society's infrastructure can also deprive people by leaving them stranded. The loss of bus services, falling employment and closures of local shops can make poor people in some rural communities far 'worse off' even if their incomes remain nominally the same. New kinds of technology and services, like computers and electronic communications, can put the poor at a disadvantage as citizens or school parents.

At what level should a 'participation' standard of income be fixed? Peter Townsend's national poverty study covered a list of sixty indicators of the 'style of living' of the population. They included diet, clothing, fuel and light, home amenities, housing facilities, the immediate environment of the home, the characteristics, security, general conditions and welfare benefits of work, family support, recreation, education, health and social life. Some indicators – like rarely eating meat or poor housing conditions – will obviously be correlated with low incomes. But low income might not prevent someone going out in the evening or having children's friends round to play. In fact, however, the correlation between nearly all indicators and different levels of income and resources was found to be highly significant. It was difficult to establish from the data a 'threshold' of income below which different people's standards of living suffered disproportionately, but the evidence suggested that wage-earners fall below a 'participation' standard of living at about sixty per cent of the average level of male wages and that state benefits would have to be raised by about half as much again to begin to give pensioners and families without a wage-earner the opportunity to share in community life (and by more for families with teenage children and people with disabilities).

The equilization of earnings

Our long-term objective is to bring about, through agreements reached nationally, a progressive narrowing of the range of pre-tax incomes, allowing for local or industrial wage-bargaining within that range. Chapters 3 and 4 commented on the huge disparity of earnings in Britain – the gap between the pay, fringe benefits and perks of the best-paid managers and élite professionals and the wages of manual workers. Inequalities in pay are portrayed by the media as the inevitable outcome of market forces, whereby the highest paid are supposed to contribute most to society and, by implication, those who are paid least are those who contribute least. However, the 1979 British election study found that a clear majority of manual workers, and a comfortable majority of Labour supporters, agreed that it was very or fairly important to 'redistribute income and wealth in favour of ordinary working people'. It is up to the labour movement to put forward proposals, which could be properly worked out and argued as the basis for positive action by a Labour government.

One major objective must be to raise low wages up to a minimum wage, equivalent to two thirds of average male earnings, in the lifetime of a Parliament. This level of earnings represents the level necessary to meet our participation standard. If all other earnings remained unchanged, this step would in itself add about three per cent to total wage costs in the economy as a whole.

The other major objective must be to win support for a maximum income limit, equivalent, say, to four times the average wage – and even that would be around £28,000 a year in 1981. The campaign for this proposal should make it plain that the salaries of the highest earners above such a limit are not justified in economic terms. They are normally determined by the highest earners themselves or by their colleagues without reference to 'market forces'. They often reflect the public image the company wants to portray.

A maximum income limit would be the most important step towards a general narrowing of inequality of incomes and raising low wages and benefits. The earnings of those at the top in the City, industry, commerce and elsewhere influence the whole hierarchy of earnings in the rest of their organizations and in society at large. This is why it is important they should be controlled.

Towards a national minimum wage

Trade unions have given increasing attention to minimum wage targets. In the mid 1970s the TUC adopted a level of two thirds of the median wage as its target. We prefer to adopt two thirds of 'average' earnings – a higher target – as these reflect resources for each person rather than a notional person at the midpoint in the present unequal distribution of earnings. The problem is that many of the lowest paid, like most workers in shops, catering, clothing and textiles, are not within the scope of trade union bargaining. Thus, for all the sustained pressure by many unions, the relative earnings of the lowest-paid workers were much the same in 1980 as they had been in 1880. Experience in other countries as well as in Britain suggests that a national minimum wage and equal earnings for women (the two objectives are of course connected) can only be achieved through legislation – though obviously legal action will not be successful without the agreement and involvement of trade unions.

We have suggested that a future Labour government should set the objective of achieving the full operation of a minimum wage equivalent to two thirds of average male earnings in five years. Progress towards this objective in each industry should be determined annually by collective negotiation between unions, employers and the government, and it should be enforced by law. This would provide an opportunity for trade unions to help improve the pay and conditions of workers who, because of the structure of the industries in which they work, have difficulty in organizing themselves to bargain effectively. Progress towards the national minimum would take account of the particular conditions of the different low-paying industries. Individual workers would be able to take action through unions or individually to enforce their rights.

Existing wage councils which cover ill-organized, low-paying industries should be reconstituted and given new terms of reference conforming with the minimum wage objective. Much wider publicity would have to be given to the minimum standards of pay and conditions set for each occupation and industry and additional government wage inspectors would be needed to ensure the standards were complied with. The rights of workers in small businesses to join trade unions and seek their help in enforcing minimum standards and bargaining for improvements would have to be protected, and the government should contribute to a trade union development fund to finance recruitment activities by unions in badly organized industries. Finally, a 'fair wages law', similar to the fair wages resolution operated in the public sector (and to schedule 11 of the Employment Protection Act abolished by the Thatcher Government), should provide legal backing for workers to have their pay brought up, on appeal through a trade union, to the general level for those doing similar work in other firms.

Only with a framework of this kind is it realistic to

suppose that collective bargaining could be made effective in all industries and occupations and that workers in disorganized sectors would have any real incentive to join trade unions to secure and build upon basic legal minimum provisions.

There are fears, even within the labour movement, that many jobs would be lost if minimum wages were enforced. Yet while it is quite true that, if one employer raises wages much above the average paid by competing firms, the jobs in that firm could be put at risk, that risk is minimized if all employers are obliged to pay reasonable wages. Customers may have to pay a bit more for what have been low-paid services. In some cases there would be a long-term contraction of the service in question, but this could and should be matched by expanding job opportunities elsewhere. If low-paid work is a form of 'concealed' unemployment, the remedy must be found, not in perpetuating low pay, but in the creation of new, more productive jobs as part of our policy for full employment.

An income ceiling
In 1965 Peter Shore obtained a second reading in Parliament for a private member's Bill which, as well as requiring disclosure of top salaries, would have established a 'higher incomes council' responsible for giving advice on 'the appropriate level of emoluments in different enterprises either for individual directors and other corporate officers or in regard to the aggregate amount paid to such officers in particular companies'. The recommendations of this council, once accepted by the government, would have had the force of law. Any individual receiving more than the amount specified would have been subject to a fine and would have been required to repay the excess income to the enterprise or enterprises from which it had been received. Recent experience of commissions such as the Top Salaries Review Body or the Royal Commission on the Distribution of Income and Wealth casts doubt on the likely effectiveness of such a council unless it were buttressed in law by a definition of maximum earnings.

189

A ceiling for top earnings must be introduced carefully. The government would have to win and retain public support for such a radical restructuring of the spread of higher incomes. The rich and powerful would inevitably campaign, using the media, their own enterprises and their friends in the higher echelons of the civil service, to resist proposals to cut their income. The government would be accused of destroying incentives, of malicious envy, of undemocratic expropriation. They would say that government was out of step and that the most valuable and talented people in our society would be forced to emigrate. There would certainly be a good number of highly publicized and well-known 'exiles'.

The basic issue would be whether people really want a just society or not. Ninety per cent of the people living in Britain have nothing at all to lose themselves from a ceiling on high incomes. Only about half of one per cent would be directly and substantially affected. Some of those with incomes well above the average but below the ceiling, including many in the professions and in management, might find their privileged position eroded a little as the whole spread of high salaries and earnings was compressed.

If we want fair opportunities for all in our society it is no good having a stratosphere of very rich people setting styles of extravagance for all the others to hanker after. The biggest problem about eliminating very high incomes is in fact the extent to which we are used to accepting norms set by the most privileged. A large proportion of those who go on television are already members, or hope soon to become members, of the top income club. It will not be easy to find many of our society's traditional public figures, other than a few bishops, MPs and trade union general secretaries, who are willing to speak out in favour of an upper income limit.

A radical approach to taxation

It is important to grasp that through one device or another even our present form of society involves and requires a huge process of redistribution of income. Up to one third of the total value of production is needed for business investment and for the whole range of public services – the police, armed forces, fire services, roads, rubbish disposal, health, education and public administration. All this is financed from profits, rents, taxes, charges and so on – and properly so. Many on the right suppose that the 'productive' private sector carries the 'burden' of taxes required to finance 'dependent' public services. The fact is that the productive side of the economy does not carry many of its real costs. The public sector provides most of the infrastructure on which industry relies – roads, the railways, energy, and so on. The state educates most of the private sector's future workforce. The social security scheme and NHS bear the costs of injury, disablement and illness brought about by employment. Fewer than half of the members of our society have full-time jobs. If those not working are to enjoy anything like the same income as those in work, a further large proportion of national income has to be set aside for them. At present the process of redistribution from those at work to others is very complicated indeed. Part goes through national insurance contributions and payment of social security benefits. Part goes through contributions to private pension and insurance schemes. Apart from this, taxes help to fund interest paid to individual and institutional savers. Companies and individuals pay and receive interest and dividends not only within Britain but to and from other parts of the world. There are major, but changing, processes of redistribution within families. Parents mostly support their children, husbands to a varying degree support their wives and vice versa. Despite all these complex processes of redistribution of income, what results is ultimately unfair and unequal.

Without the tax system and national insurance things would be rather worse. But tax and insurance themselves have become so complicated and contentious that their basic purposes are generally lost sight of.

For the present, we need a tax and insurance system,

not only to reduce inequalities between those who earn income, but even more to fund public services and to provide for all those who do not earn income, whether because they are too young, too old, disabled, unemployed or for other reasons. In the next chapter we shall argue for a comprehensive welfare system providing benefits for all who are not at work. If state benefits are to reach our participation standard of income, they require a very large revenue. For example, if the majority not at work were to receive on average an income level equal to two thirds of the net income of those at work, about thirty-five per cent of the total national income would need to be set aside for this purpose. Taking investment and public services into account as well, people who 'earn' income could on average retain only about one third of the value of what they produce. But of course they would benefit from higher-quality public services and a higher standard of living when they no longer work.

The fact that a large proportion of national income needs to be redistributed, and would need to be so even if earnings were equalized, is one which we cannot afford to obscure. Any presumption that taxation and other deductions from the income generated by production are 'artificial' or unnatural flies in the face of reality. The greater part of income is and should be social in nature. Tax allowances and tax exemptions which most people, especially those with higher incomes, tend to regard as their natural prerogative are in fact a major reason why redistribution in our society remains so inadequate.

To make the tax system fair and effective it is plainly necessary that all income should be covered. Wages and salaries, investment incomes, capital gains (after taking account of inflation), fringe benefits and private pensions should all be included in taxable income, and all taxed in the same way.

The key to radical reform of the tax system lies in phasing out the network of tax allowances and reliefs which we described in Chapter 4 and reaching a collective decision on two fundamental points – the level of the participation standard we want the state to guarantee for all members of our society, and the degree to which we want the tax and insurance system to bear more heavily on high earnings than on low earnings. If the pattern of earnings, including not only pay but fees and income of all other kinds, were fairly negotiated in the framework of a minimum wage and the income ceiling discussed earlier, it would be reasonable to abolish tax allowances and reliefs altogether in favour of a uniform deduction on all earnings, whatever their source. In the long run, taxes could be paid entirely by firms (and the self-employed) and pay could be conceived of and bargained in net-of-tax terms.

The counterpart of a broad tax and insurance system without allowances and exemptions must of course be a system of cash benefits and subsidies that is extensive and flexible enough to cope with the full diversity of people's needs. Pensions and child benefits are only the beginning of such a system. To escape from means tests and the use of benefits as an instrument of oppression and social control, the basic level of benefits payable on simple criteria such as age, sickness or unemployment needs to be much increased. A miser's welfare state is bound to place many people in a situation of having to ask for more and being subjected to humiliating and arbitrary judgements.

What the labour movement should press for, therefore, in conjunction with minimum wage provisions and a ceiling on high incomes, is the phasing out of tax allowances and reliefs in favour of a fully developed system of cash benefits. In the process, tax and insurance deductions should be brought towards a uniform rate. People at work, instead of suffering a complex and little understood system of levies, contributions and tax deductions, some formally paid by the employer and some recorded on their pay slip, should come to expect that a major part of the income generated by their enterprise will go to fund investment, public services and social benefits. The remainder, accruing to them as net pay, should be subject to no special deductions at all.

The socialization of wealth

The most fundamental problem of all is the extreme concentration of most personal wealth in the hands of a tiny proportion of the population. Death duties and gift taxes have done almost nothing to reduce this concentration of wealth and attempts to introduce a wealth tax have been frustrated. The concept of an upper ceiling to income, discussed above, would put very large personal holdings of wealth immediately into question since the owners would effectively be disbarred from receiving any income accruing from their wealth, beyond the income ceiling. But the ceiling would not prevent them from wasting their excess wealth, for example by extravagant spending, or from using it as a source of personal power.

In fact wealth raises issues of power and responsibility which are at least as important as the link between wealth and income. Here we shall argue that the main objective with regard to concentrations of personal wealth should be to bring the resources in question into forms of social control or common ownership.

This objective does not make effective inheritance taxes and an annual wealth tax unnecessary. On the contrary, if concentrations of private wealth are to be brought into social ownership, there will have to be effective instruments for obtaining the transfer. The point is rather that instead of thinking of wealth in an abstract way and then running into difficulties on real questions like the management of land, shares and even historic houses and works of art, we must envisage and argue for the removal of concentrations of personal wealth in terms of the institution of new, more accountable ways of exercising the power and responsibility which the possession of wealth affords to our society. Professor Sandford recently identified three reasons for the failure of the last Labour Government to introduce a wealth tax: 'Lack of research and preparation; apathy among many Labour MPs; and, above all, the failure of the party to develop any coherent philosophy on the distribution of wealth.' The last of these problems is the one that we shall discuss here.

The establishment presents proposals for reducing the concentration of personal wealth as a threat to businesses, farms and our national cultural heritage. They suggest that a wealth tax would destroy wealth. But the objective of socializing wealth implies nothing of the sort. The aim is in fact to extend access to the services which wealth can render. Farming need no longer be a monopoly of the rich. Recent research shows that many small and moderate sized farms can be more efficient than a few large ones. Alternatively, cooperatives can run large farms very efficiently. Through cooperatives, far more people could have opportunities to participate in the management of businesses. Stately homes and parks could provide leisure facilities to the community at large.

The socialization of wealth is a process which has gone on, to some extent, through a long period of history. We no longer live in a world dominated by feudal barons or owner capitalists. Wealth is held in increasingly indirect forms of which pension and insurance funds are a particularly important example. Millions of people in this country have pension or insurance rights through funds to which they regularly contribute. The pension funds in their turn own blocks of shares in companies which have many shareholders. The companies, finally, own the real property, in the form of land, equipment and stocks of materials and goods which are the ultimate 'backing' for individual pension and insurance rights.

Even very rich people today typically hold much of their wealth in a financial, and therefore indirect, form. They own shares, government stocks and bank accounts. This exempts them from most of the responsibility involved in the management of real wealth. People used to be shocked if a landowner ran down, or sold off, an estate to pay for extravagant living. It is somehow more legitimate for the modern rich with their paper wealth to waste income and assets on their personal whims and fancies, since the connection between their actions and the real wealth they indirectly own is so oblique.

The indirect and dispersed ownership of wealth gives

huge and concentrated power to the small class of top managers in industry and the City who manage wealth on behalf of others. We have already suggested that the power of decision now wielded by this class needs to be made far more broadly accountable both to democratic government and to collective bargaining in its various forms. It is also part of our proposals that the widely extended, but all too arbitrary and inadequate, mass of pension and insurance schemes should be brought progressively into an extended and comprehensive national system. This in itself would remove the putative ownership of a large proportion of shares and other financial assets from the beneficiaries of the pension and insurance schemes.

The transfer of shares and other financial assets owned by pension and insurance funds into the hands of the government would render the stock exchange as a 'capital market' more or less inoperative. Therefore it seems sensible that as pension and insurance funds were brought into a national scheme, personal holdings of stocks and shares should also be brought within the same system, being exchanged in the most part for entitlements to future benefits on some progressive scale.

Personal holdings of land and real estate such as rented housing should also be brought into forms of social ownership. The capital even of small businesses, over a low minimum threshold, could be provided through forms of social equity. In the long run there should not be much reason for anyone to need to hold personal wealth outside their home and bank account. Nor should there be any need for the productive assets of our society to be managed by rich private owners.

We must therefore envisage on the one side periodic wealth levies taking major proportions of concentrations of personal wealth into common ownership, and on the other side the development of institutions of social ownership capable of managing effectively the personal wealth which is taken over. The socialization of particular forms of wealth could involve varied forms of compensation, depending on the circumstances of the owner and the nature of the wealth. Private pension and insurance rights could be exchanged for rights in the national insurance scheme. Shares belonging to ordinary people could be exchanged for cash or insurance rights. Shares belonging to very rich people could be set against their liabilities under a wealth levy without the need to pay compensation.

The process of ridding our society of the antique hierarchies of wealth and property rights by which it is permeated will sometimes be difficult and complicated. But once we evolve principles for common ownership and provide the legal framework for putting them into effect it will be perfectly feasible and realistic to phase out traditional laws and institutions of property and in the same process displace personal wealth from its present central role in our society.

14 Social services for all

The achievement of social equality depends upon the development of a more generous and universal system of social security and social services, and upon strengthening the powers of the local community within that system. The strategy has to be universal: that is, rights and opportunities in pensions, social security, housing, education, health and other services must be enlarged and made accessible to the entire population. Means tests for public benefits and services within the welfare state; private and occupational benefits and services, distributed by the market according to people's ability to pay; and powerful bureaucratic and professional structures, both public and private, all have to be disentangled from British life. Means-tested benefits do not reach millions of people who are nominally eligible for them; private welfare is massively subsidized through tax reliefs of all kinds, trust law and charitable status. Together, they act like a cancer, destroying human fellowship, fair shares and freedoms, and confirm a class-fractured and irresolute society.

A transformation of the welfare state to meet our universal ideals would necessarily involve the reduction and eventual abolition of private and occupational welfare. The very point of its continued existence is to buy advantage at the expense of the majority of people. No government, however, can ban overnight all private and corporate welfare. An incoming Labour government could begin to shake the golden bough by gradually withdrawing the indirect state subsidies on which the private sector feeds and by publicly earmarking the revenue regained for the restoration of the welfare state. It should initiate an immediate review of trust and charitable law to root out the class privilege which is poorly disguised as altruism. It must, however, be recognized that progress would be slower on some fronts than on others. It would, for example, take longer to change the law of charity to remove the financial advantage of charitable status from private hospitals and public schools than to end their exemption from VAT. The government would have to take account of the natural anxieties of beneficiaries and, for example, phase out tax reliefs so that people's lives are not disrupted. It must be recognized that many workers gain a benefit – dubious and double-edged though it often is – from being allowed to share in the bottom end of the private welfare market. This is not an argument for masterly inaction: it is an argument for change which is responsive as well as purposeful. The case for that change is powerful and it should be put. Real progress in ending private advantage in welfare depends on building a popular and informed consensus for change – and, most fundamental of all, on making genuine advances in the quality and accountability of public benefits and services which extend a sense of security to all. In this chapter, we consider how ending private privilege and expanding public services might go hand in hand.

Recasting the welfare state

A universal strategy also means that the income needs of the employed, and non-employed people dependent on state benefits, should be decided according to a common body of principles. Big differences in living standards between earners and non-earners are too often condoned. Through the state, the public has been invited to decide what benefits should be available to people who are out of work, or too old or sick to work, rather than what incomes are needed in comparable circumstances by those both in and out of employment. We argued in Chapter 13 that social control of the unequal wage structure would not only benefit the low paid, but would allow higher benefits to be paid to people who were not receiving salaries or wages. We further recommended that tax allowances should be recast as cash allowances.

One of the major advantages of this switch from 'invisible' to 'visible' benefits is that it would allow a socialist government to disentangle decisions about the level of support received by families with children, invalids or other dependants from decisions about the level of earnings. Men's earnings are, for example, still often negotiated on the notion that they are the breadwinner's contribution to keeping a family. But wages are simply not flexible enough to provide for an average number of children in a family: in practice, no wage earners actually have 2.4 children, and while millions have no children at all, some thousands have six or more. A cash benefit – in this case, the now familiar child benefit – provides flexibility and would, unlike wages, concentrate help where it is needed.

We have already expressed the hope that a Labour government would take into accountable common ownership the semi-socialized wealth of the pension funds and insurance companies, and so transform it into fully socialized wealth. This would allow the government to create a truly universal social security scheme, which actually would meet the high standards which the Beveridge Report aimed for, but failed to realize. It could provide protection for every crisis in life from the cradle to the grave: maternity, disability, sickness, unemployment, dependency, single parenthood, widowhood, old age and death. It could even, if people wanted to incorporate them in a universal scheme, include house, fire and other types of insurance. This means that a future Labour government would have to abolish the contributory principle which provides such an inadequate base (as we have demonstrated in Chapter 5) for the existing national insurance scheme. And even if the government failed to take over pension funds and insurance societies, it should make the abolition of the contributory base a founding principle of a recast social security scheme. All state benefits would then become non-contributory and, in the first instance, would be financed more equitably than now entirely out of general taxation (though firms and organizations would continue to pay contributions to the cost).

Fair shares for families

One of the central objectives of a recast social security scheme must be to give families with dependent children sufficient financial and other support to allow both parents full opportunities to share in the care of the children, and to fulfil themselves in work and in their social and community life; to give extra assistance (and priority while resources are limited) to free single parents to participate more fully in work and life outside the home; and to relieve the social disgrace of poverty which has increasingly been concentrated among families with children. In our view, British society fails to give due weight to the needs of young children and their parents; and, in particular, remains too willing to consign women to isolated, non-cooperative work in the home. Higher child benefit represents the first, and most major, step towards this objective. A child benefit which actually met the cost of keeping and bringing up a child would entirely separate the issue of family support from decisions about the level of wages, and would allow the government to equalize the child benefit paid to parents, irrespective of whether they were working or not. An increase in child benefit is also the most immediate and effective way of reducing family poverty among those in work, and would begin to disengage these poorer families from the stigma of means-testing and the disincentive effects of the 'poverty trap', which we described earlier. It would promote better diet and health, meet the additional expenses of children in a changing society, and raise the only independent source of income which many mothers have. Higher child benefit would further restore greater equity of living standards between young adults with children and people in middle age. Over time, this would represent not so much a redistribution of resources between different groups in society, but a shift in resources over people's life cycles.

At what level should child benefit be fixed? It has been estimated that the cost of a child rises from about 6.5 per cent of average male earnings for a two-year-old to over nine per cent at the age of eleven. Teenage children plainly cost more, but how much is not known. Our view is that child benefit should vary with the age of the child, but for the sake both of simplicity and equity, we recommend that the first goal of a Labour government should be to raise them to the level of child allowances paid with long-term national insurance benefits, which this year were equivalent to nearly nine per cent of average male earnings, then index-link them to earnings. Finally, however, they should more accurately reflect the cost of bringing up children; a higher rate would then be paid for older children (with similar rises in the supplementary benefit rates).

Labour is already committed to higher child benefit. But this should simply provide the floor for a vastly improved system of family support. It is often not appreciated how badly Britain has fallen behind other European countries in social concern for the family. Other countries have infant care allowances, widely accessible day care for the under-fives, rights to long-term maternity and/or paternity leave (which are sometimes interchangeable to allow either parent to care for the newly born child) and substantial maternity grants and pay. Infant care allowances are to be distinguished from child benefit: they are paid to compensate for the earnings which are lost when a parent has to care for a dependent child, or to fill out the income of a single parent. We should like to see a scheme for care allowances introduced in Britain, and weighted towards the care of dependent children under five years old. As a priority, we would award care allowances for every child aged under three. In the first instance, these allowances would be payable to a family, even if no one stayed at home to care for the child: the principle would be to allow parents to choose whatever mix of paid day care and part-time or full-time care in the home suited them. If, over time, society in general decided that day care should always be available free, then it would be proper to continue the allowances as a recognition of the work which personal care involves, and to break down the divide between caring for dependants and paid employment.

As we have already proposed, in Chapter 13, the new family care allowances we are advocating should be financed in part by the withdrawal of personal tax allowances. The first to go should be the married man's allowance, which is currently (1981) worth about £4.50 a week to married couples on the standard rate of tax. This benefit is received not only by couples with young children who are being cared for by a wife who does not work outside the home, but by 1.5 million couples (or more usually men) without children. Those with several children and those with none receive the same benefit. Since parents with young children at home need a much more generous level of support, its abolition in exchange for care allowances makes for both sense and equity. Other personal tax allowances – like the additional personal allowance, age relief, single person's allowance and personal allowance – can also be progressively abolished in exchange for cash benefits to pay for the care of children, disabled relatives, invalids, the elderly infirm and other dependants in the home. Incomes below the participation level would be exempt from income tax. This process has to be linked to the precedents set by attendance allowances and invalid care allowance (for the care of severely handicapped people). We see this as a logical development to raise the incomes of non-earners and especially to begin to establish better rights for many women not currently paid for the care they undertake. In the end, equity between them and those in paid work has to be achieved.

As we later explain, we are wary of imposing too great a central control on local authorities, but minimum standards for certain services must be established. Among these services is universal day care for the under-fives. An adequate day care service would allow parents to mix family care, work and social and community life as they wish, and would further provide a social environment within which young children could develop. Additionally, the statutory period for maternity leave needs to be extended – say, to eighteen weeks as a first stage – and made interchangeable with paternity leave. These are the kind of formal measures a democratic socialist government might take. It is to be hoped that there would be corresponding changes at the workplace, with flexible hours, part-time work and job sharing all made more widely available. Here much would depend on changes in attitudes among employers and employees, and among men and women. The overall objective for the labour movement and any Labour government must be to provide the framework within which men and women could achieve a satisfactory integration of family life and work and to allow women genuinely to achieve equal opportunities with men.

The difficulties of one-parent families would be greatly alleviated by all these measures – and since most one-parent families are headed by women, they would be further relieved if our earlier proposal for a national minimum wage were carried through. Nevertheless, a lone parent is plainly at a disadvantage by comparison with a couple who can share the tasks of caring and earning, and some kind of extra benefit needs to be provided to lift single parents who are not in full-time work out of the supplementary benefit scheme. In the long run much would depend on introducing systems of taxation, social security benefits and care or home responsibility allowances on an individual rather than a 'married' basis. But to establish the material basis of equality between the sexes is likely to take time and until then single parents should receive a benefit which is equivalent to widowed mother's allowance. If the single parent benefit lasted for a year, regardless of a change in circumstances, and was renewable by way of a sworn statement by the claimant, testifying to solitary household and financial status, the draconian impact of the cohabitation rule would be mitigated, and the rule would be one more of independent financial status.

Better pensions for all

The last Labour Government's superannuation scheme, with earnings-related state pensions yoked into an unequal partnership with occupational pensions, was designed to provide a lasting bipartisan case for future pensions policy. As we have seen the scheme confirms existing inequalities between pensioners through tax reliefs and state supplements for inflation. The scheme does nothing to raise the living standards of poor retirement pensioners – who form a majority of the elderly population – and not much for those who are in sight of retirement. But over sixty per cent of the workforce are in occupational pension schemes, and so have an apparent personal interest in their survival.

Occupational funds are, however, vulnerable on many fronts. As we have pointed out, their investment record has generally been prejudicial to the interests of British industry, though profitable for the City institutions. The performance of the funds is poor. They are heavily dependent on tax reliefs at almost every turn. The employees who put their savings compulsorily into the funds have scarcely any say in how they are managed (few large funds even have a formal fifty-fifty representation for employees). Being long-term funded schemes, they are inflexible and might well not be able to cope with changes in the age and structure of the workforce, or changes in people's expectations or in social policies. They are inequitable, even among their own beneficiaries. Many workers have rights only to very small weekly pensions. Most important of all, though their spread through the workforce seems to give them strength, their great weakness is that they are tied to work, and almost invariably to a single place of work. Thus, they only apply to half the population, and only few of them get full pensions: those who remain with the same employer for most of their working life. Pension rights cannot be transferred from one employer to another. The large-scale redundancies of the past few years are demonstrating cruelly how real a liability this is.

A Labour government intent on radical reform should,

at least, withdraw tax relief on contributions to occupational pensions; insist on full transfer rights; make the pension funds responsible for their own index-linking; and give employees real power over the management of the funds. It should at the same time act to improve the basic retirement pension for existing pensioners, and publish plans for the long-term future of state pensions. In this way it should remove the fear of poverty in old age which has encouraged the unions to bargain for occupational pensions as an alternative to state pensions at subsistence level only. This strategy would leave the way open for real bargaining between the government, unions, employees and employers over the future of occupational pensions, and should make the advantages of a universal state scheme clear.

The most urgent priority is, of course, to raise the value of the basic, or flat-rate, state pension to lift existing pensioners out of the need to apply for supplementary benefit (or supplementary pension, as it is known), and in particular to give a decent standard of living to the million or so retired people who are entitled to supplementary pension but fail to apply. The retirement pension for single people and couples should be raised to the participation standard we described in Chapter 13, and the rates for the very elderly could be supplemented to allow for their extra needs. Had this standard applied in November 1980, the basic pension at sixty-five would have been £36 a week instead of £27.15. Those who become disabled would also qualify, like younger people, for additional disablement and attendance allowances. This advance could in a small way be paid for by the withdrawal of tax reliefs on individual private pension contributions, the abolition of the right to draw tax-free lump sums on retirement, and measures to prevent high-paid managers from avoiding tax on their salaries by 'salary sacrifice' schemes which defer payment until after retirement. Once the basic pension is raised to a more adequate level, index-proofing must be restored for *all* pensioners.

These measures would provide the coping-stone for

living standards in old age. But while we choose to give weight to the improvement of basic pensions for existing and future pensioners, we would keep the earnings-related state scheme, but with no contracting out. By raising the basic rate of pension and providing for earnings-related supplements, the way is open for most of the occupational schemes to be accommodated within the universal state scheme, without any loss of expectation to the pensioner on retirement, and in most cases with enhanced security. While we believe that there would be strong support for a reduction overall in equalities in earnings, we realize that there is public and trade union support for some acknowledgement of differentials in skills and qualifications and in working conditions, with some desire that this might be reflected in pensions. Moreover, many workers have built up contributions to an additional pension over many years, and accumulated entitlements must be honoured, at least up to the level of the new state earnings-related scheme. Secondly, opportunity could be afforded through voluntary contributions to augment the earnings-related pension through a state-run scheme. A second-tier ancillary scheme would offer money-purchase benefits. The benefits paid out would depend on a person's contributions and the rate of return on these investments over time. If other schemes did remain on the market, a state-run scheme could provide a much better rate of return – given the unnecessarily high administrative costs, high brokers' fees and premiums, and promotional and other costs of the present pensions and insurance industries. These benefits would become standard entitlements for all citizens who reach pensionable age. Over time, this age should become sixty for both sexes, but retirement should not be imposed on individuals.

Towards a disability income
Disabled people deserve a new deal. For any government, the introduction of a comprehensive disablement allowance for people of all ages should be a priority. At the

moment, someone who has been injured at work or in the armed forces receives generous compensation, according to the degree of disability, through a weekly allowance, plus an income from work or invalidity or other benefits. But someone who is born with the same degree of disability receives only the low non-contributory benefit. A comprehensive allowance would end such inequities and turn an anomalous patchwork of benefits for disabled people into a coherent and defensible scheme. Allowances would be paid according to a scale of rates which reflected the degree of disability and how far it limited a person's activity. The highest rate would be the same for all those most severely disabled, irrespective of whether their disability was incurred through industrial injury, war, an accident at home or on the roads, a chronic disease or a congenital handicap. Physically disabled, mentally handicapped and mentally ill people would all be equally eligible for allowances. Disabled people in work or on other benefits would continue to qualify for an allowance, according to the severity of their handicap: the principle should be that the allowance is paid to meet the additional expenses of their disability and to provide compensation. A comprehensive scheme would be expensive, and organizations of the disabled themselves have advised that it should be introduced by stages, beginning with the most severely disabled on the highest rate. If this rate were equivalent to the top rates for war and industrial injury pensioners – as it should be – the first stage of a new scheme would have cost £120 million this year.

Important though it is, a comprehensive disablement allowance will not of itself give disabled people the full membership of society that they demand. Nor even will improved services – though many disabled people and their families would prefer more widely available services to extra cash. Such services include day centres, home helps, adaptations to their homes, holidays. There has to be a change in attitudes, not simply among public and private officials but among the public. Opinion polls show that people are overwhelmingly in favour of providing adequate benefits and services for the disabled, but less willing to accept their fuller integration into the community. A greater familiarity with disabled people is most likely to foster their wider acceptance in the community. And the most appropriate way forward would therefore be to push ahead with a more thoroughgoing integration of physically and mentally handicapped children in ordinary schools, a continuing switch from institutional to community care for many handicapped adults, and a strengthening of the quota scheme for the employment of registered disabled workers.

Unemployment and sickness

Higher child benefits, a disablement allowance and a universal pension scheme represent the three key measures which would be necessary to make a reality of social security through the state. Our economic and industrial policies are designed to greatly diminish the number of unemployed workers and to expand employment, and hence should make unnecessary massive funding for unemployment benefit. However, the general thrust of our proposals would have to be maintained for unemployment, sickness and other benefits. The most important remaining change in the existing scheme would be to make unemployment benefit last as long as the need exists. Unemployment and sickness benefits should also be raised to the participation standard we set for wages and pensions.

Equality between the sexes and races

Equality in social security cannot be obtained independently of equality in employment, and in taxation. A number of specific proposals listed earlier for employment and taxation would benefit women. The Sex Discrimination Act does not cover social security and pensions, just as it does not apply to taxation. Married women suffer discrimination because they are treated as dependent on their husbands for the purpose of state benefits. However, women can claim a state retirement pension at sixty while men must wait until they are sixty-five and widowers have weaker rights than widows to benefit. Social security law should be revised to ensure equality, and seek progressively to move towards treating men and women as individuals with equal rights. This would involve equity of entitlement between widows and widowers, a common benefit rate for men and women irrespective of dependency, and equal conditions of entitlement to benefit. Married women with disabilities would have the same rights as others with disability.

In the same way as for women, our proposals are intended to provide such a powerful redefinition of universal rights that public, local or private discrimination against those belonging to racial minorities would be greatly diminished. We believe that a strategy of prevention – through the positive implementation of principles of social equality and equal individual access to services – is preferable to self-conscious action concocted on behalf of labelled racial minorities. The establishment of universal rights to employment, adequate wages and social security, and health, welfare, housing and education is the true path to racial equality. We acknowledge, however, that there is a strong case for policies of 'positive discrimination' to overcome the handicaps from which women and blacks now suffer in employment, education and other areas, and a future Labour government should consult with women's organizations and representatives of racial minorities to consider what policies of 'positive discrimination' might have to offer in the short run.

A fair deal for housing

House and home stand at the centre of people's lives. The first aim of a socialist housing policy must be to ensure that everyone in the community has a home at a cost they can afford. In the longer run, we would want to give people a free choice in determining the standard and location of their home, and between owning individually or cooperatively and renting housing of equal standards and status. These objectives cannot be achieved without reducing and redistributing the massive tax subsidies to owner occupation and devoting a substantial proportion both of the savings and of the higher public spending we advocated earlier to investment in building new public housing and rehabilitating existing rundown public and privately owned properties.

Equity between private ownership and public renting should be strenuously pursued. The profit motive must be removed from owner occupation by immediately abolishing mortgage tax relief at the higher rates of tax paid by the rich; reducing over time the period for which relief can be claimed to ten years; and bringing privately owned housing within the scope of wealth and capital gains taxation. Such measures would be misrepresented as an attack on owner occupation.

In fact, while they would undoubtedly restrict the privileges which the richer home-owners enjoy, they would concentrate financial assistance for home buyers where it is most needed – in the first years of a mortgage – and by bringing about a fall in house prices, would also help the first-time buyer as against the established owner occupier. House buyers could also be helped by the abolition of stamp duty – an arbitrary and unfair levy; by price controls on estate agents' fees and alternative municipal and cooperative house exchange services; by a crash programme of land registration to simplify house buying (a system not unlike log books for cars could then be introduced); and by ending the solicitors' monopoly in conveyancing.

The changes should make it possible to give public housing equal status with owner occupation. New standards of space, amenities and access to play areas and gardens would have to be determined. Central cost controls, which have forced councils into building inferior housing with high maintenance costs, need to be removed. Council housing should no longer be pushed into the less attractive areas. Tenants' rights should be determined on a body of principles and standards, which give tenants freedom equivalent to those in the private sector. Most fundamentally, effective control needs to be transferred from paternalistic management to locally constituted tenants' councils, composed of directly elected tenants, housing staff, representatives of the local community and councillors. Real budgetary and management powers could be devolved to such bodies; and they, in turn, ought to be obliged to report fully on their activities to local tenants and residents.

Britain's housing stock is deteriorating faster than it is being repaired and replaced. A substantial proportion of new housing investment must therefore be directed towards rehabilitating properties which are falling into obsolescence, including 'hard-to-let' council estates, old privately rented property in the inner cities and, increasingly, houses owned by low-income, and especially pensioner, households. A Labour government should immediately extend security of tenure in the privately rented sector; and to avoid the high immediate costs of acquisition, councils could be given vesting powers to take control of neglected privately rented properties which they plan to repair and improve. Owners would be entitled to annual payments, equivalent to a fair return from renting. In the long run, all rented accommodation should be publicly or cooperatively owned. Public investment through improvement grants to owner occupiers should cease, for they are effectively subsidies from the taxpayer to already well-off house buyers or to private landlordism. They should instead be replaced by loans which, if need be, could be repaid only when the property is sold or the occupier dies; but many elderly owners would prefer simply to switch over into sheltered public housing. They should be able to do so.

It seems wrong that people should be entitled to buy second homes when some families are homeless, or that building resources should be used to extend and to build spacious homes when other houses are in desperate need of repair and amenities. We hope that the labour movement might build up a popular consensus that control of second homes should be imposed in areas of housing shortage; and that a future Labour government might gain assent for restrictions on certain types of building activity. That government will also in the short term have to defend the principle that public homes should be allocated on a fair system of priority needs, and will have to extend this principle to allocations of mortgage funds by building societies. The simplest immediate answer might be for the societies to make a fixed percentage of their mortgage funds available for lending by local authorities, with full guarantees for the security of their loans. In the longer term, the conscious aim of socialists must be the achievement of a surplus of good housing where it is needed. Only this will allow for real freedom of choice in housing; and only this will finally liberate public housing from the constraints of scarcity and allow it to play a full role in meeting people's needs.

An education for participation

The kind of society we envisage will require a far higher standard of general and political education than exists today. Education would be regarded as a preparation for a fulfilling personal life, for democratic practice, and for participation in the life of the community, socially, culturally and politically. Education of this kind would recognize a wide diversity of gifts in their own right – as the best comprehensive schools already seek to do. Indeed, only comprehensive state schools can make higher general standards of education available free and as of right to all. By the 1970s, most major industrialized nations had advanced or were advancing comprehensive education past the primary stage into secondary schools to raise the standards of the majority. In Britain, that advance has been obstructed by the continued existence of the core of élite public and private schools, and by political battles to retain selective schools within the state system. In many ways surviving grammar schools reflected and reinforced the narrow public-school ethos. Decisions about the organization of secondary education have been dominated

213

not by issues of the quality of secondary education, but by a class-based concern to defend privilege and power.

We need to abolish private schools which perpetuate class privilege, and to create a genuinely comprehensive system of nursery, primary and secondary education. It is at secondary level that most needs to be done. Our objective must be to provide a broad, basic and high-quality course for everyone, without streaming. The organization of schools must, however, also be flexible enough to cater for all types of ability and intelligence, mental and physical handicap, and differing social and religious customs and beliefs; and though secondary schools should all be 'neighbourhood' schools, it might be necessary to have some degree of specialization among them. The common curriculum must break down the bias towards narrow and specialized academic disciplines which reflect the class-based dominance of professional people in later life. This bias creates among the majority of children who fall out of such academic study the feeling that they have somehow 'failed', and inhibits them from developing their own abilities and exploring their creativity.

The Labour Party has long been embarrassed by its commitment to abolish the public schools. But a more purposeful approach is now evolving, and the party's National Executive and the TUC General Council have recently agreed a detailed set of proposals to bring private education to an end. The central proposal – to make the charging of fees for new pupils illegal – would of itself take time to carry through, and would almost certainly inspire a long drawn-out legal campaign in defence of private education. At the same time, however, a future Labour government should implement measures agreed in the joint policy document to withdraw state aid from private education. The Conservative assisted places scheme – under which a token handful of children are educated at public schools with financial assistance from the state – should be abolished. Charitable status – and the tax advantages and rate relief which accompany it –

should be withdrawn from private schools. Their exemption from VAT should be brought to an end. Local authorities should be prevented from buying places at public schools and government boarding allowances for army officers and diplomats should be abolished. State-trained teachers should be obliged to do their first years of teaching in state schools (and, in our view, public schools could be levied to meet the costs to the public of training their staff). Private schools which could be put to community use should be integrated into the state system (through enabling legislation if need be). Finally, an alternative school commission could be set up to encourage experimental schools within the public sector.

In some countries, open access has even reached the universities. We should merge together sixth forms, colleges of further education, universities, polytechnics and adult education, and so seek to create comprehensive education past the age of sixteen. We devalue both our language and political system when we describe as 'youth opportunities' dead-end tasks for unemployed teenagers like clearing cemeteries or counting a town's dustbins. A future Labour government must fulfil its manifesto pledge to provide a universal scheme of education and training for all sixteen- to nineteen-year-olds which is flexible enough to meet a diversity of needs and aspirations through two- or three-year block courses, or day or block release over a similar period or longer. We fall badly behind other industrialized nations in our training for young people. There should be negotiations, industry by industry, to expand apprenticeship schemes and to secure their joint financing by government and industry. The present confusion of child benefit (paid to parents), means-tested local allowances for poor school pupils, grants for further education, supplementary benefit for unemployed youngsters and token wages for those on job creation schemes, all paid at differing levels on different criteria, needs to be rationalized into a universal scheme of grants for education and training which recognizes young people's need for independence. At university level, it is difficult to justify investing large sums on only a very small proportion of the population. All people should have the right to some time off in their lives for education or training, and especially at critical times, such as a return to work after child-rearing, on redundancy, or at the end of a career. Grants could be made available, and those who did not take advantage of the scheme could retire early.

Finally, schools should be made genuinely accountable to governing bodies, with directly elected representatives of the local community, parents, teaching and other staff, and (at secondary level) pupils. Parents should all be more closely involved in the work of the school. The newly merged sixth form and further education colleges, polytechnics and universities should also be made more broadly accountable than they are at present. Academic freedom must be preserved, and indeed extended, but it must not be used as a shield for unaccountable and hierarchical palaces of privilege paid for out of public funds.

Reduction of inequalities in health

In promoting the nation's health, two fundamental changes in perception are necessary. One is to recognize the limited role of the health and welfare services themselves and to call attention to the importance of measures to raise material standards of living as experienced by working people at work, in the home and in everyday social and community life. Doctors, nurses and others working for the NHS should be encouraged to recognize this necessary condition for the success of their own more specialized work. It is through general action to eliminate deprivation and promote social equality that the most dramatic improvements in the nation's health can be achieved – as was copiously illustrated in Britain in the 1940s.

Second, we need to adopt a positive rather than negative interpretation of 'health'. It is not enough to develop services concerned only with curing illness, or restoring the body's physical and nervous system to reasonable functioning. We have to learn how ill-health can be prevented and good health promoted, and how human energies and emotions can be satisfyingly mobilized in a full life. So far the NHS has concentrated on healing disease once it has developed. Efforts must increasingly be made to catch illness early or to prevent it – through, for example, screening and anticipatory action by food and work safety inspectorates. People can also be encouraged through more effective health education to understand the combined value of good diet, physical exercise and beneficial conditions at work, in the home and in the environment.

Two sets of policies derive from these perspectives: more radical preventive action against the tobacco and drug companies; the establishment of minimal amenities of work and work conditions, and control of dangerous products, especially as they pollute the environment and increase the chances of disease. Homes made uncomfortable by motorways and dangerous, intrusive or noisy forms of industry would have to be rebuilt elsewhere. Play space for young children, outdoors as well as indoors, day nurseries, leisure and sports facilities should become widely accessible – and be regarded as part of the 'social wage'. Community health service should be strengthened and the integration of doctors into community health teams accelerated. Preventive health strategies need working out at this level, preferably with young families, people with disabilities and other consumer groups being involved in preparing and monitoring the strategies. At the moment, the bulk of national resources in money and manpower is invested in hospitals (for example, more than sixty per cent of qualified doctors work in NHS hospitals), so that curative, as distinct from preventive, medicine and acute illness, as distinct from chronic illness or disability, are given disproportionate attention in the range of health care service. We recommend a redistribution of resources for the antenatal and postnatal services, health visiting and family planning and welfare centres; new incentives, especially for doctors, to work in areas with too few health workers; and dramatic improvements in the numbers and conditions and range of work of home helps, community nurses and other community health workers.

We also propose that target dates be laid down for the achievement of substantial coverage of each local population for elderly, disabled and mentally ill and handicapped people. Costly hospitals for mentally handicapped patients should gradually be phased out in favour of sheltered housing, family group homes and small hostels. Other long-stay patients ought to be cared for in similar settings, though some would need to be in small community hospitals or residential nursing homes under the general care of specialists such as geriatricians or psychiatrists. Far fewer elderly and disabled people would then need to be in residential homes, and priority could be given to sheltered housing and specially designed individual housing in every neighbourhood.

The case for a universal approach to health services is both strong and widely accepted. The growing privatization of medical care begins by allowing the better off to jump the queue and will end by excluding those who most need it from the best care. A Labour government would probably not be able to ban private hospitals and medical care (partly because the NHS has shamefully neglected some services, like abortion facilities, and ignores certain types of treatment). It could, however, introduce a levy on private hospitals to help pay the cost of training doctors, nurses and other staff, and bring tax concessions (including the exemption from VAT) and then charitable status to an end. It should also outlaw all private treatment in NHS hospitals and begin negotiations with the doctors and dentists to create a salaried public service within the health service, and withdraw the new tax allowances on private medical insurance. These measures in themselves would provoke the most bitter and obdurate resistance from the professional bodies, running even to the danger of mass resignations from the service. It is possible, however, that the medical profession's representative bodies have overreached themselves: their arrogance and avarice have been well publicized. A Labour government which was determined to regenerate the NHS, and willing to devote extra resources to doing so, should be able to mobilize public backing for measures which were designed to restore its founding principle: 'To ensure that everybody in the country – irrespective of means, age, sex or occupation – shall have equal opportunity to benefit from the best and most up-to-date medical and allied services available.' Those are the words of the coalition government's white paper in 1944. It might also assist a Labour government's cause if it were at the same time to bring forward proposals to decentralize and democratize the health service.

Belief in community

Our proposals would bring about a dramatic improvement in the quality of life of the local community. Integral to them is the principle that local people must be able to share in the decisions about how social security and other services are organized and delivered. The culmination of the measures we have described and the democratic processes by which they might be implemented is not easy to anticipate. The regeneration of the local community would spread far beyond local government to the workplace and all local organizations. This regeneration would not merely be a by-product of the structural change we envisage, but would represent one of its essential elements. More equal earnings would be reflected in more collaborative forms of work organization, with the worker having the opportunity of performing different roles – not a restricted or narrowly repetitive one. That seems a logical corollary of wage equality.

But greater reliance on the general skills of the mass of the population and their natural resourcefulness would also diminish the pressure for the perpetuation of unequal educational and social status and for highly specialized and sometimes artificial forms of training. This would strengthen the case for a much higher level of basic education for everybody, both in childhood and at later stages of life. It should also lead to the diminution of professional and bureaucratic power, and perhaps to fewer professionals and bureaucrats. The mass of the people would be more involved than they are at present in what is going on around them, and would acquire a greater range of skills. The scope for having more control over their lives at school, in college, at work, in the home and in the local neighbourhood and community (as well as nationally) would be enlarged. At the same time, people's sense of fellowship, as distinct from their individualism or class membership, is bound to be heightened. While the rules for the production and distribution of resources would have to be sanctioned nationally, the principles of social justice and more equal shares logically entail that more power will be devolved to the local community, and to individual people in that community. They would share in decision-making, nationally and locally; and, equally, they could come to depend for support on a network of community self-reliance. Harnessed to the principles of democratic involvement, socialism can enrich individual and family life within the community. Local organization and community can become the building blocks of democratic socialism in a self-confident and powerful society.

Index

accountability 157, 174–7, 199
  civil service 96–9, 148–50
  courts 88–9, 160–61, 164
  government 90–95, 147–8, 164–5
  information control 81–3, 89, 152
  Labour Party 114–16, 128, 132
  peerage 95–6
  police 85–8 *passim*, 100–103, 169–60
  security services 83–5, 158–9
  trade union 129, 171–2
Acts of Parliament
  Commonwealth Immigration
    (1962) 72
  Education (1944) 42, 68
  Employment Protection (1976) 70,
    188
  Equal Pay (1975) 70, 71
  Immigration (1968) 72
  Nationality (1965) 163
  Official Secrets (1911) 78, 79, 92,
    115
  Prevention of Terrorism (1974,
    1976) 87
  Public Order (1936) 86
  Sex Discrimination (1975) 70, 209
  Vagrancy (1824) 87, 94
'advanced capitalism' 22
aid programmes 18–20
alternative economic strategy 132–4
  implementation 138–43
  main differences 135–7
  planning programme 136, 143–6
armed forces 103–4
'asset-stripping' 37–8
attendance allowances 203, 206
authoritarianism 77–9, 90–95, 111,
  180
  in judiciary 99–100
  and information control 152

Bank of England 33, 37, 38, 98
banks and banking 23–6, 31, 32, 140
benefits 183–4, 192–3
  contributory principle 60–61, 200
  visible and invisible 199–200
  see also individual benefits
Beveridge Report (1942) 60–62, 200
Britain 21, 134
  authoritarianism in 77–9
  deindustrialization of 29–30, 142
  relations abroad 17–19, 21, 180–81
  representative government in 90–104
  role of City in 31–41
  socialist 129–31

Bullock Committee 168, 170
'Butskellism' 42, 44, 110

cabinet committees 95, 97, 115
capital, free movement of 22–
  7 *passim*
capitalism 22, 128, 130, 141
care allowance (infants) 202–3, 204
child benefit 63, 193, 200–202, 204
citizenship status 72, 83, 163
City of London 133
  economic power 31–8 *passim*, 196
  Labour government and 38–9, 43,
    55, 133, 140
  political power 31, 39–41
civil service 39–40, 78, 79
  power of 96–9
  recruitment 97–8, 115, 149–50
  role, in open government 148–50
class privilege 105, 108–10, 118–19,
  122
  civil service structure 97–8, 149
  education 33, 49–50, 67–70
  inequalities 42, 43–5, 63–4, 125
  judiciary structure 99
  peerage and 95–6, 113
  private welfare 45–51, 58, 198–9
  revisionism and 111, 113
collective bargaining 167–71 *passim*,
  173, 175–6, 188
'combine committees' 173
common ownership 166–7, 194, 196–7
  role and accountability of 174–7, 200
community health service 217–18
community self-reliance 157, 219–20
corporation tax 53–4
Court Report (1976) 64
courts
  class structure 99–100
  politics of 88–9, 96, 99–100
  reform of 160–61
credit restrictions 135, 145–6, 178
currencies, value of 26, 30

decision-making 36–9, 219–20
democracy 123–4, 126–7
  government reform 147–8, 151,
    164–5
  labour movement 129, 132
  legal system 158–64
  local authority 155–7
  media and 153–5
  participatory 150–51
  see also industrial democracy

democratic socialism 131, 153, 167
devaluation of pound 111, 112, 137
directorship 33–5
disabled people 208–10
  benefits 60–61, 63, 74, 203, 206–9

ecology movement, socialism and 130
economic growth 43–4, 110, 185
economic planning 177–81
  see also alternative economic strategy
education 42, 45, 67–70, 97, 99
  accountability of schools 216
  comprehensive 68–9, 213
  nursery 69, 71
  public school 33, 49–50, 51, 113, 214
  standards 74, 213–14
  and training scheme 215–16
EEC 13–15, 22, 111, 134, 135
  Britain and 18–19, 21, 115, 136, 137,
    139, 140, 141–3
  revisionism and 112–13
employment
  discrimination 70–73
  full 112, 113, 134, 137–9, 189
  see also unemployment
equality
  before the law 162–4
  planning for social 150–51, 179
  in social security 209–10
  socialist programme 123–5
  see also inequality
ethnic minorities 120–22
exchange controls 133
exchange rates 26, 139, 140, 145–6
exports 20, 142

family support 42, 60, 62–3, 193,
  201–4
free trade 14, 20–23, 29, 111
  see also international trade
fringe benefits 44, 47–9, 56, 186, 192
  cost of 50–51
Fulton Committee (1966–8) 97

GATT 16, 22, 24, 140
government 14, 15, 21
  accountability 90–95, 147–8, 164–5
  authoritarianism 77–9, 90–95, 111,
    180
  City influence 31, 34, 37, 38–41
  economic control 24, 26–7, 133–4,
    140–41, 144–5
  information control 78–80, 83–5
  open 147–8, 152–3
  representative 90–104
  role 131–2, 179–81
government reform 147–8, 164–5
  civil service role 148–50, 153
  disclosure of information 152–3
  legal system 158–64
  local authority proposals 155–7
  media's role 153–5

parliamentary role 151, 152
social planning/equality 150–51

Half Our Future (1968) 67
health care
  NHS 42, 45, 51, 55, 58, 63–5, 75,
    216–19
  private 51, 55, 58, 218
Home Secretary 84, 100–102, 159–60,
  163
House of Commons 91–4 *passim*, 96,
  115
  government reform and 151, 152
House of Lords 91, 95–6, 99, 100, 113
  abolition of 116, 151
housing 65–7, 210–13
  council 65–7, 73–6, 211–12, 213
  private 45, 46, 50, 57–8
  racial discrimination 73–4

IMF 16, 22, 24, 26, 30, 43, 113, 136,
  140, 142
immigration control 72, 83, 120,
  163–4
imports 20, 23, 137, 144
  British dependence 29, 112, 139
  control 133, 140, 141, 146
income, distribution, *see* inequality;
  wealth
income tax, *see* taxation
incomes policy 111, 112, 137, 140,
  146
  'voluntary' 113, 117
industrial decline 14–16, 18–19, 135–6
  centralized power 32–3
  City influence 34, 37–8, 112
  conflicts and crises, resolving 144–5
  internationalism and 14, 22–3, 29–30
  Labour's strategy 128, 167, 179–81
  regeneration 133–4, 138–9, 143–5
  underinvestment 112, 135
industrial democracy 113, 145, 146
  collective bargaining 167–71 *passim*,
    173
  common ownership 166–7, 174–7
  company negotiations 172–3
  development of 169–71
  see also nationalized industries
inequality
  disability benefits 60–61, 207–8
  educational 67–70, 213–16
  health 63–5, 216–19
  income 44–5, 183–4, 186–93 *passim*
  racial 72–4, 210
  reinforcement 45–51
  sexual 72–4, 210
  taxation 51–4, 56, 58
  see also class privilege; equality
inflation 14, 22, 66, 135, 139, 140
  alternative economic strategy 145–6
  recession and 28–9, 43, 44
information disclosure 152–3, 157

industrial 169–70, 173, 176
  state controlled 81–5, 89, 92–3
insurance 31, 32, 33, 195–7, 200, 218
  medical 48–9, 50–51, 218
  national, *see* national insurance
international trade 15–16, 18–19
  dominant role 26–7, 180–81
  European interdependence 141–3
internationalism 13–15, 22–6, 134–7
invalid care allowance 203
investment 36–9, 112, 133, 135
  proposals 138–9, 144, 174

judiciary, *see* courts

Labour government 38–9, 42, 43, 48,
  50, 53, 131–2
labour movement
  alternative economic strategy 132,
    133–4, 138–46
  declining support 105–8
  democracy within 129, 132
  and industrial democracy 167–9
  media and 129, 130, 132
  organizational conflict 105–6, 113–
    16, 127–8
  trade unions and 105, 107, 108, 113–
    14, 127–30, 141, 143
Labour Party 37, 42, 53, 55–8
  democracy within 121–2
  future of 118–19
  industrial strategy (1975) 136
  minority groups 119–21
  revisionism 105, 106, 110–113, 118
  socialism 108–10, 111, 127–9, 130
  trade unions and 116–18
law, equality in 162–4
law and order consensus 79–81
legal aid scheme 162–3
legislation 93, 94, 95–6, 153
  see also Acts of Parliament
Lindsay Report 82
living standards, participation 184–6,
  187, 192
'lobby' system 41
local authorities 75, 131
  services 76, 135, 203–4
  strengthening democracy of 155–7

market system 27, 30, 135, 136, 141
  planning role in 177–9
maternity rights 70, 71, 202, 203–4
means-testing 55, 60, 62, 198, 201
media 34, 40–41, 66, 153–5
  labour movement and 129, 130, 132
Ministers, role of 148–9
mixed economy 111, 113, 137, 167
  common ownership in 174–9 *passim*
mortality rates 63–4
mortgage tax relief 57–8, 66, 98, 211
multinationals 13, 23, 28–30, 112,
  134, 135

City's role 31–32, 34, 36–8

national insurance 42, 55
  inadequacies 59–62, 200
  and tax reforms 191–3 *passim*, 197
nationalized industries 90–91, 107–8,
  110, 116
  closures 135, 175–6
  see also common ownership
NATO 13, 16, 19, 21, 103, 111
NHS, *see* health care
Northern Ireland 79, 82–3, 87, 104,
  159

OECD 16, 19, 22, 53
official secrets 78–9, 83–5
oil 18, 19, 22, 26, 27–8, 142
Ombudsman 93, 157, 160
one-parent families 59, 61, 63, 201,
  202, 204
OPEC 19, 22, 26, 28
open government 147–8, 152–3, 180
  see also government reform

Parliament, *see* House of Commons;
  House of Lords
'participation' standard of
  income 184–6, 187, 192, 203, 206
participatory democracy 150–51
pension(s)
  funds 31–2, 37, 133, 195–7, 200, 205
  occupational 46–7, 50, 205–7
  private 44–5, 58, 207
  proposals for state 193, 205–7
police
  accountability 85–8, 100–103, 159–60
  powers 80, 82, 83, 85–8, 89
  Special Branch 82, 85, 103
policy decisions 90–95, 126–7, 130
  civil service power 96–9
  and information control 152–3
  Labour movement 114–16, 121–2,
    129
  in open government 148–50
  peerage power 95–6
  police 102
politics 123, 128
  armed forces and 103–4
  Britain's role 15, 16
  City influence 31, 39–41
  court system 88–9, 96, 99–100
positive discrimination 210
poverty 14, 59, 60, 201
  line 54, 60, 62
  participation standard 184–6
  trap 55, 56–7, 201
power 128, 194
  City 31–41 *passim*, 196
  civil service 96–9
  government 91–5, 131, 140–41,
    147–8
  local authority, extending 155–7

power *continued*
  peerage 95–6
  revisionist theory 110–11
  trade union 116–18, 172–3
powers, negative (obstructive) 126–7
preventive medicine 216–17
production 138–9, 144, 177
profit 53–4, 137
  financial logic of 36, 37–8
  subordinating 136, 175, 177
public expenditure
  cuts 28, 30, 43–4, 55, 56, 64, 74–6, 113, 135, 136
  cuts (campaign against) 123, 131
  increase proposals 133, 138–40, 143
  revisionist theory 110–11, 113
  social equality and 150
'public order' 86
public services, accountability of 199
  see also individual services

racial discrimination/disadvantage 72–4, 83, 95, 120, 163–4, 210
recession 27–30
  see also alternative economic strategy; industrial decline
retirement 44–5, 125
  see also pensions
revisionism 105, 106, 110–13, 117, 118, 121
rights/freedoms 77–8, 85–7, 125–7, 168

security services 83–5, 158–9
select committees 94–5, 97, 149
sick-pay schemes, private 46, 47
sickness benefit 209
Social Democratic Party 106, 114, 118, 122, 137, 174–7
social control, democracy of 158–64
social needs 25, 113, 136, 150, 184–5
social policy, joint approach 150–51
social security 42
  benefits 43, 44–5, 201–10
  limitations 59–63, 76
'social wage' 43, 217
socialism 129–31
  common ownership goal 166–7
  Labour's 108–10, 118, 123–9
  response to economic crisis 131–2
socialization of wealth 182, 194–7, 200
Special Branch 82, 85, 103
sterling 39, 117, 139, 140
stock exchange 39, 196, 197
subversives and subversion 84, 103
supplementary benefit 60, 61, 62, 136

taxation 42–3, 55–8, 156
  allowances (in cash) 199–200
  avoidance 43, 44, 53, 56

income redistribution 35–6, 44–8, 66, 67, 183–4
  progressive 43, 44, 51–4
  reform proposals 190–93, 203
  revenue from 30, 136
  revisionist theory 110, 113 *bis*
  'tax expenditures' 50–51
  wealth 53, 113, 194–5, 196
technology 24–5, 29
Third World 19–20, 28
trade and industry planning 143–4
trade unions 42, 113, 130–31, 168–9
  accountability 129, 171–2
  company negotiations 172–3
  labour movement and 105, 107, 108, 113–14, 116–18, 127–30, 141, 143
  minimum wage target 187–9
Treasury 92, 98–9, 150
TUC 116, 172, 187

under-fives 69, 71, 202–3, 204
unemployment 14, 15, 22, 25, 128, 136
  benefits inadequate 59–60, 61, 62, 209
  minimum wages and 189
  racial disadvantage and 73
  recession and 27, 29, 43
  revisionist theory 112–13
United States 16, 22–3, 27, 111, 185

wage(s)
  control, *see* incomes policy
  equalization of 186–7, 199–200
  national minimum 187–9, 193, 204
  upper limits 189–90, 193, 194
wealth 35–6, 111, 194
  indirect forms 195–6
  socialization of 182, 194–7, 200
  tax 53, 113, 194–5, 196
  see also inequality; wage(s)
welfare, private 43, 45–51, 58
  abolition/reduction of 198–9
  welfare state cuts and 74–6
welfare state 15, 29, 58, 128, 136
  cut backs 15, 43–4, 74–6
  development 42–3
  expansion 198–200
  social security proposals 201–10
  see also individual services
Western Europe 18–23 *passim* 27, 141–2
women 59, 68
  discrimination 70–72, 95, 187, 204, 209–10
  in Labour Party 119–20
  non-working 42, 61, 201, 203
workers' cooperatives 174, 176, 195
working class, labour movement and 106–10